ROUTLEDGE LIBRARY EDITIONS:
SOVIET POLITICS

Volume 25

THE WAY OF BITTERNESS

THE WAY OF BITTERNESS

Soviet Russia, 1920

PRINCESS PETER WOLKONSKY

with an Introduction by
COL. JOHN BUCHAN, M. P.

Routledge
Taylor & Francis Group

LONDON AND NEW YORK

First published in 1931 by Methuen & Co. Ltd.

This edition first published in 2024
by Routledge
4 Park Square, Milton Park, Abingdon, Oxon OX14 4RN

and by Routledge
605 Third Avenue, New York, NY 10158

Routledge is an imprint of the Taylor & Francis Group, an informa business

© 1931 Methuen & Co. Ltd.

British Library Cataloguing in Publication Data
A catalogue record for this book is available from the British Library

ISBN: 978-1-032-67165-9 (Set)
ISBN: 978-1-032-67622-7 (Volume 25) (hbk)
ISBN: 978-1-032-67626-5 (Volume 25) (pbk)
ISBN: 978-1-032-67624-1 (Volume 25) (ebk)

DOI: 10.4324/9781032676241

Publisher's Note
The publisher has gone to great lengths to ensure the quality of this reprint but points out that some imperfections in the original copies may be apparent.

Disclaimer
The publisher has made every effort to trace copyright holders and would welcome correspondence from those they have been unable to trace.

THE WAY OF BITTERNESS

THE FIRST COUNT BOBRINSKOY
MY GREAT-GREAT-GRANDFATHER (1762–1813)

THE WAY OF BITTERNESS

SOVIET RUSSIA, 1920

BY

PRINCESS PETER WOLKONSKY

WITH AN INTRODUCTION
BY
COL. JOHN BUCHAN, M.P.

WITH FIFTEEN ILLUSTRATIONS

METHUEN & CO. LTD.
36 ESSEX STREET W.C.
LONDON

First Published in 1931

PRINTED IN GREAT BRITAIN

TO

HER HIGHNESS

PRINCESS MARIE LOUISE

WITH SINCEREST THANKS

INTRODUCTION

IN May 1919 the author of this book managed to reach Finland from Russia, and journeyed thence to England to see her daughter, leaving behind her husband, who was subsequently arrested and imprisoned in Moscow. The life at Bath was a strange contrast to the terrors of the Soviet régime; but England could be no continuing country for one who had left such a hostage behind her. She decided to return, and somehow or other to secure her husband's release. First she tried to enter through Finland and failed, but in the end she succeeded by way of Reval. She followed the advance of the White Army, and, when it was driven back, went on to Petrograd on foot. In Petrograd, where lay her bedridden mother-in-law, she was without passports or identification papers, and in constant danger of her life. With the help of Maxim Gorky she obtained a passport and reached Moscow, where her husband was imprisoned. Then began months of such suffering and struggle as few women can have endured. In the end by sheer persistence she succeeded in getting her husband released, and the two went to Petrograd, where she worked for her living as a doctor. Her problem was now how to leave Russia, and at last, after heart-breaking delays wife, husband, and mother-in-law reached Esthonia.

The book is the most vivid picture I know of the chaos of Russia in 1920—the hunger, the forced labour, the crumbling of all humanity's foundations. Princess Peter Wolkonsky uses language as a weapon of precision, and her little sharply-etched pictures are more terrible and more memorable than a library of high-coloured rhetoric.   But the supreme merit of the book is the story—a story of heroism and fortitude which almost surpass belief.   They must have been extraordinary indeed to have melted the heart of Dzerjinsky.

It is a book which I hope will be widely read in Britain, for it is a proof to what heights human nature can rise.   The tale of the Russian exiles since the Revolution is a wonderful record of patience and dignity in suffering.   The Russian temperament has always been credited with the courage to endure, but this book shows that it can rise also to supreme courage in action.

JOHN BUCHAN

NOTE

THIS story—which I first called *Vae Victis*, and still think of under that title—is true.

I have invented nothing. I have not even exaggerated or adorned. I have told the things that have happened to me, the things I have seen and heard. A few names have been altered—for more or less obvious reasons. That is all.

S. W.

LIST OF ILLUSTRATIONS

THE
WAY OF BITTERNESS

CHAPTER I

MAY 1919. A muddy little river, a few armed soldiers, a bridge—the border-line between Russia and Finland. I stand there hesitating, uncertain. The same old doubts assail me. . . . I am still on Russian soil, there is still time to turn back. Only a few steps across the bridge; but how hard it is to take them. They mean so much.

However, time is up. My decision is made. I cannot miss the chance that has been given me; one is not twice offered the opportunity of leaving Soviet Russia unmolested.

Only a few steps. . . . There. . . . It is done. I am over. The Rubicon is crossed. I am now in Finland. Russia is behind me—Soviet Russia. I am in a free country, among normal people. I ought to feel happy. But my heart is heavy: Pierre, my husband,[1] has remained on the other side.

---

[1] Prince Pierre Wolkonsky, former diplomatist, Secretary to the Russian Embassy in London, Berlin, and Vienna.

I

Ten days of quarantine in Terioki. Divers coming up from great depths under the sea are not allowed to come straight to the surface, but have to pass first through a series of chambers in which the pressure is gradually decreased ; the human organism cannot bear too sudden a contrast. People accustomed to the life of Bolshevik Petrograd could not be dropped without some transition into the gay atmosphere of post-war Europe. It would, however, be erroneous to ascribe the quarantine restrictions to nothing but kind solicitude on the part of the Finnish Government ; the measure had been prompted much less by the fear of overtaxing our hearts than by the desire to protect the country against the poison they possibly contained. Under the label of sanitary quarantine, a search was being conducted for the bearers of Bolshevik microbes and a line drawn between innocent victims and smugglers of incendiary ideas. A kind of customs inspection where instead of tea, cigars, or scent you were asked to declare your juvenile enthusiasms, your communist affinities, or dreams of an Utopia on earth.

Long, monotonous days full of idleness and tedium : no books, no interesting conversations—nothing. My only comfort was the telegram I got in answer to my inquiries, telling me that after the Crimea had been evacuated, my daughter [1] and her grandmother [2] had reached England on board a

[1] Princess Sophy Dolgorouky, my daughter by my first marriage, then aged twelve.

[2] Princess Olga Dolgorouky, mother of my first husband.

British man-of-war, and were now living somewhere near London. Anxiety for my daughter, the horror of complete uncertainty as to her fate after the fall of the Crimea, were the only reasons that had made me leave Russia. Now that I knew she was safe, why not turn back at once ?

Hour after hour I sat gazing at the waves of the Finnish Gulf. At night the lights of Kronstadt were visible. How near we were to Petrograd ! When I closed my eyes I could see so distinctly our little white house on the Fourstadtskaia. What are they doing there now ? I wondered. Because of the house with all its memories, my mother-in-law had refused to go abroad ; to leave the country meant to abandon one's home to destruction. And Pierre stayed because of his mother, who was old and suffered from deafness. ' You must understand,' he said, ' that I cannot abandon Mother here to face the revolutionary turmoil, alone in the house with the servants. Whatever happens, I must remain by her side.' While she said : ' Il faut croire en la miséricorde de Dieu ' ; or else, ' Tout va changer ces jours-ci avec l'aide de Dieu, pourquoi risquer des difficultés plus grandes par tes extravagants projets.' The *extravagants projets* consisted simply in leaving the country after having sold the few valuables that were still in our possession.

My arguments, my entreaties were powerless to move her. *Il faut croire en la miséricorde de Dieu.*

She was adamant. It ended by my going abroad alone, while my mother-in-law and Pierre remained in Petrograd.

Helsingfors. All those who succeeded in getting out of Russia during the first years of the revolution remember the joy they experienced at the sight of open shops, restaurants, theatres—all the outward manifestations of European civilization. No display of luxury in the windows of Bond Street or Fifth Avenue ever provoked such spontaneous delight as that given us by the smallest Finnish shop. The pangs of bodily discomfort are as a rule easily forgotten ; but none of us, I am sure, will ever forget the animal joy of the first square meal after months and months of semi-starvation, the greedy thrill born at the sight of a real English cake ! What a shock it was to meet a stout man in the street ! Fat people are the emblem of a prosperous country ; you never met one at that time in communist Russia.

The foreign newspapers interested me at first nearly as much as the grocery shops. What did they say about Russia ? Did they bear out the rumours that had circulated all last winter in Petrograd concerning the coming foreign intervention ?

A short time ago, here in Paris, while looking over some old letters, I came across several notes that Pierre and his mother had written to each other

MY DAUGHTER SOFKA, AT THE AGE OF EIGHT

during that winter ; although living under the same roof, they were in the habit of sending short messages from one end of the house to the other. In one of these notes, dated as far back as January 1919, she writes to tell him all the latest political news that had just reached her through the gossip of a neighbour :

' Les blancs sont à Volosovo, près Gatchina, Mannerheim en tête qui amène du pain à Petrograd. Schlusselbourg est pris ou plutôt occupé par l'escadre anglaise. . . .' [1]

All of which was, naturally, quite wrong ; the White troops were at that time many miles away from Gatchina ; while Mannerheim, the Finnish Dictator, unfortunately never was at the head of any army marching against Petrograd ; had he done so, events might have taken a very different turn. As to the British Fleet—it was then, as it remained for us to the end—nothing but a beautiful dream.

A week later it was Pierre who wrote :

' Radkevitch [2] reoptimiste parle de la prise de Pskov (!) par les blancs et de nouveau d'un terme de deux à quatre semaines qui pourrait amener libération.' [3]

[1] ' The White Army is at Volosovo, near Gatchina, led by Manner-heim, who is bringing bread for Petrograd. Schlusselbourg is taken, or rather occupied by the British Fleet.'

[2] A. A. Radkevitch, of the Russian Foreign Office, died in a Bolshevik prison about a year later.

[3] ' Radkevitch, once more in an optimistic mood, says Pskov (!) has been taken by the ' Whites ' and speaks anew of a period of two to four weeks as liable to bring us liberation.'

Rumours that the Allies were soon coming to rescue Russia had lately grown more and more persistent ; some people had even seen—seen with their own eyes—the smoke of British battleships near Kronstadt. . . .

I opened the papers in the hope of finding, if not direct confirmation, at least some veiled hints on the subject. Starting first with the local papers, I next read those from Stockholm, lastly *The Times* and the *Matin*. There was of course a great deal concerning the Peace Conference. All eyes were directed towards Versailles, where the Big Three sat composing the victor's bill, summing up the costs, and trying to express the value of a few million human lives and four years of inhuman suffering in terms of gold marks and square acres. Turning the page I came upon an account of the races at Newmarket, the list of winners in a tennis tournament. . . . There was an article on the ' Causes of the World War ', and several items of news that struck me as remote and uninteresting. Hardly a word about Russia. A few lines in one of the big papers, that was all.

So much for the smoke from the funnels of the British warships near Kronstadt !

Helsingfors, Stockholm, London. . . . The invasion of Europe by Russian fugitives was already in full swing ; everywhere I met old friends and acquaintances. I was one of the last to have left Russia

and was assailed on all sides for news from home.
' How soon will the Bolshevik régime fall ? ' was
the chief question. Nobody doubted that it could
only last a few weeks, a few months at most. My
timid scepticism evoked nothing but smiles. Nearly
all those I knew led a comfortable, care-free life,
pawning their last jewels and hardly giving a thought
to the problem of to-morrow, so sure were they that
the present state of things in Russia was on the eve
of collapse. It is easy to criticize now ; at the time
I was hardly wiser than they. The absurdity of
communist theories as a practical creed, the unheard-
of cruelty of the régime—all seemed to guarantee
its near end. Civilized Europe could not possibly
abandon yesterday's ally, leave her to perish at the
hands of a small group of fanatics put into power
by a scheme devised in Berlin ! Only very few of
us knew better ; it was a short time after the advent
of the Bolsheviks that Prince Youri Troubetskoy
said to me : ' Mark my words—it is going to last
ten years.' His prophecy sounded to me then as a
silly joke.

At a big dinner in Stockholm I met an old friend,
the Spanish diplomat Aguerra. He had been
appointed Ambassador to Russia shortly before the
October revolution, but having been unable to reach
Petrograd in time, was now awaiting the restoration
of a normal Government. He was living in Sweden
so as to be nearer his new post, which he hoped to

join as soon as the long-expected *coup d'état* took place.

London.   Uncle Sac has taken me a room at the Ritz.   Oh, the joy of luxury !

My stay in London was short.   I was in a hurry to join my daughter at Bath.   It was my first visit to Bath, and I fell at once under the charm of the quaint old city, for ever steeped in its dreams of past splendour, haunted even now by the shadow of Beau Brummell.   All was neat and clean, the same as everywhere in England ; splendid old oak trees, velvety lawns, beautiful roads, and an all-pervading atmosphere of quiet tedium.   One could hardly have found a spot more soothing to the nerve-racked ' victims of the revolution '.   I found my daughter much grown ; it was nearly a year since we had parted.   And what a year !   She too had had her full share of exciting experiences : the occupation of the Crimea by the Bolsheviks in 1918, the arrival of the Germans, then a new advance of the Reds, causing general panic among the inhabitants and a wild flight from the peninsula.   My daughter and her grandmother were embarked on board the *Marlborough* in the suite of the Dowager Empress. From that moment they were out of danger.[1]

[1] It is impossible to speak of those events without mentioning the courageous act of the Empress, who refused to depart until all fugitives had been given a chance of leaving Yalta.   It was not then, but at the second evacuation of the Crimea, that so many were left behind to be murdered savagely by the Bolsheviks.

ON BOARD THE 'LORD NELSON', 1919

H.M. THE LATE DOWAGER EMPRESS, GRAND DUCHESS XENIA, PRINCESS DOLGOROUKY (SOFKA'S GRANDMOTHER), SOFKA, WITH HER DOG, MISS KING, AND OTHERS

Sofka had been impressed above all by the scene
of a night search at their country house in Miskhor,
conducted by a party of Bolsheviks, with two sailors
the worse for liquor, brandishing their revolvers in
the face of the old Princess and repeating : ' Don't
be afraid, madam. Don't be afraid.' Miss King,
Sofka's governess, was very proud of her pupil's
display of fortitude ; having attached herself to
Granny's skirt, she never left her for a moment
until the end of the unwelcome visit.

One feels curious about the educational results
of such an intrusion of life into the nursery. What
will become, I wonder, of these children whose first
memories are not nursery games and fairy-tales but
tipsy sailors and revolvers ?

' When I was young,' said Princess Dolgorouky,
' I used to dream of the great French Revolution
and wished I could have lived in those interesting
and romantic days. Now I have learned, alas, that
revolutions are neither interesting nor romantic.'

Later she once said to me : ' Every day of my
life I have repeated the words of the Lord's Prayer,
" Give us this day our daily bread," but I never
thought the time would come when I would have
to give them a literal meaning.'

Sofka knew about my second marriage already.
Impossible as his success appeared, the messenger
had managed to reach the Crimea and deliver her
my letter announcing the event. This was by no
means an easy feat, considering the general fighting

then going on all over the country. As a result of the hardships he endured, the man fell ill with typhus as soon as he had fulfilled his mission.

Peaceful sunny days at Bath. Every morning the old Princess would go into the town and drink a glass of mineral water ; later in the afternoon we would all drive far into the country, while the evenings were mostly taken up by a game of Patience. To the eye of an outside observer no existence could be calmer or nearer the ideal state of animal placidity. But under the surface all was turmoil, at any rate as far as I was concerned. Day after day passed bringing me no news from Pierre, and my impatience, my anxiety, my fears grew with every hour. To add to my torment, vague rumours of a most disquieting nature reached us even at Bath, whilst the short communications of the Press were getting more and more alarming. A new wave of terrorism had swept over Russia : wholesale arrests, mass executions of the *bourgeoisie* were reported. . . . It was simply maddening ! How I longed for the smallest sign—just a single line—to tell me they were safe in the little white house on the Fourstadtskaia !

Out of a letter that never reached him :

Contrary to all physical laws, the force of your attraction not only does not decrease in inverse ratio to the square of distance, but the farther I go, the stronger I seem to feel it. The moment approaches when neither reason nor motherly affection will prove capable of retaining me here any longer. I deliver Fate an ultimatum : if next week brings me no good news, I take matters into my own hands.'

Naturally they all said I was mad ; at that time the idea of any one returning to Russia was in itself absurd. First of all, argued my friends, I should never be able to get through ; the frontier was closed and all communications with Russia had ceased. And even supposing the impossible—supposing I should succeed in getting to Petrograd— what help would I be able to offer ? My presence would probably prove to be only one more burden in circumstances already difficult enough, one more source of worry and anxiety. They were probably right. I did not know. Perhaps I should really be unable to get into Russia ; perhaps I could really be of no practical help. . . . Perhaps. . . . Still I could not—I simply could not—stay here any longer. I would go to Finland ; there I would be at least nearer to the Russian frontier ; from there it would be easier to learn something about events in Petrograd. I might even try and get in touch with Pierre. . . . Then I could decide what to do next.

Saying good-bye to my daughter. . . . She was happily too young to form any clear idea of what it all meant. My train left early in the morning. The Princess was still in bed when I came to take leave ; she blessed me with the sign of the cross and I left her room my eyes full of tears. Sofka and Miss King saw me off at the station.

Next followed a few busy days in London: seeing to my passport, obtaining the necessary visas, etc. I had also to choose a school for Sofka, and after some deliberation decided on Queen's College—a decision neither of us ever regretted. At Fortnum and Mason's I ordered a big box of various dry stores. Small though the chances were of its ever getting with me as far as Petrograd, I wished to make the attempt. Imagine the amount of happiness that box would give my starving friends, the splendour of the feast I would be able to offer them! Only imagine!

During my stay in London I was the guest of Prince Felix Youssoupoff at his flat in Knightsbridge. An extraordinary little flat, extraordinary surroundings, extraordinary people. The most striking feature was my host. What a fascinating personality! He knows the secret of rendering his faults as attractive as his good qualities. If not more so. . . . As if we love people for their virtues!

Many compatriots, having heard of my plans, came to me with all kinds of requests; some asked me to visit their houses in Petrograd, another had not heard for months from his old mother, and so on. I had not the heart to refuse, and without much thought promised everybody to do what I could. If only I should ever get there.

Eses came over from Paris. Eses was an old friend. The foundation of our friendship lay in the many experiences we had shared during the earlier period of Bolshevism in Petrograd, culminating in our joint arrest in the autumn of 1918, preceded by one of the most disagreeable night-searches I have ever endured.[1] Those who have never been through it can scarcely realize one's emotions when wakened by a trembling maid in the middle of the night, with the startling news that a party of Red soldiers are actually conducting a search in the next room ; emotions ever so much more intensified when at the same moment you are confronted with the problem of immediately finding a secure hiding-place for a big black portfolio containing a bunch of incriminating papers the possession of which was at the time much more dangerous than a box full of dynamite. But that, according to Kipling's famous formula, is a different story.

Eses entirely disapproved of my plans, but understood that arguments would be useless. He offered very kindly to give me a letter for L. B. Krassin, the Bolshevik commissar, whom he knew fairly well ; the connexion between those two had always been something of a riddle to me. I accepted his offer with gratitude—who could tell what difficulties were in store for me ? The help of

---

[1] Eses was at that time living in my flat, protecting it thereby, in his quality of foreigner, from the ever-present menace of a proletarian invasion.

Krassin might some day prove of the greatest value.

Here I must relate an event which although seemingly insignificant had some most unexpected and disagreeable consequences. A few days after my talk with Eses I was having lunch at my cousin's, Sophy Abeecee. Sophy's husband was at that time at the head of the naval branch of our Intelligence Service abroad. At lunch I met a colleague of Abeecee's, then on the point of returning to his post in Norway. Let us call him V. Hearing that my husband was in Petrograd, V. most kindly offered to get a letter through to Russia ; quite an exceptional opportunity, he assured me. ' You may be just as outspoken as you wish,' said V., ' for in case of danger the messenger may be obliged to destroy the papers, but he will certainly never give them up to the Bolshies.' It was indeed a most exceptional opportunity, so having expressed my gratitude to V., I sat down immediately after lunch to write my letter. Knowing it would be a long time before another such chance was given me, I wrote much more openly than usual, certainly more openly than was prudent, telling Pierre my intention of returning to Russia, and even mentioning in a guarded way the letter Eses had given me for L. B. By way of precaution I did not write the full name of Krassin, but just his initials—L.B. (Leonid Borisovitch). V. took my letter, promising once more that it would very soon be in the hands of my husband. A few days later I left London.

Eses accompanied me as far as Newcastle, where I was to embark for Sweden. I felt depressed and unhappy. What fate awaited me ? Nothing was certain. True, a fortune-teller in London had assured me that all would end well and that she could see me in London together with my husband ; but then, how was I to know whether her prophecy was based on true inspiration or simply on her eagerness to earn her guinea fee ?

The ship started at last with a great rattling of chains, to the accompaniment of the indispensable good-wishes and waving of handkerchiefs (how one hates, when young, these standardized displays of emotion !), while I stood leaning silently against the taffrail, my eyes riveted on the fast-receding coast and on the lonely figure of Eses rapidly melting into the fog.

CHAPTER II

B AD news awaited me in Stockholm. Pierre
had been arrested and put into prison. The
news had been brought by Baron Nolde, who
had just escaped out of Russia at the risk of his
life. Nolde had been arrested nearly at the same
time as Pierre ; but they had released him, whilst
Pierre remained behind the bars. As far as Nolde
could tell no accusation had been brought against
Pierre ; no trial awaited him. He was to be held
as hostage, condemned to live in prison (and what
a prison !) for an indefinite period. He would be
kept under the constant menace of one day being
taken out and shot by way of reprisal for some act
of terrorism directed against the Bolshevik leaders,
or in answer to some restrictive measure against
Communism adopted by a foreign country. Lenin
was frank enough to state outright his intention to
exterminate the *bourgeoisie* as a class. In those early
days the Bolsheviks hardly ever resorted to the mock
trials which were later staged in order to impress
gullible foreigners.

This new development, i.e. Pierre's arrest, finally
settled the question : I must return to Russia. It
was nearly impossible to get released from a Bolshevik prison without help from outside. At the

same time I learnt that the difficulty of crossing the frontier was almost insuperable. However, my English nurse had always told me that 'Where there's a will there's a way'. The next day I sailed for Finland.

In Helsingfors I immediately set to work. I had been given, more or less secretly, several addresses of men who undertook to help people cross the frontier. My object was clear : in some way I must reach Petrograd. Money I had, and neither hardships nor danger would put me off. However, the answers I received were evasive : the moment was badly chosen, the frontier had been greatly strengthened, so that even intelligence messengers could hardly pass ; the only thing to do was to wait and watch the turn of events ; would I inquire again, say in a week's time.

All right, I was ready to wait—for a short period. I even felt relatively calm, as far as calmness was possible in my present situation. Thanks to the several friends I met at the hotel (the so-called *Societatshuset*), life was made bearable. Once again I came across the Spanish Ambassador Aguerra, who had come over here from Sweden and was still waiting for his post in Petrograd to be ready to receive him ; then there was Behr, councillor of the Russian Legation at Stockholm, who helped us to while away the long, empty evenings by his clever rendering of old gipsy songs to the accompaniment

2

of the guitar.   How strange it seems that this same Behr, this gay and light-hearted companion, has now become a priest, and under the name of ' Father Nicholas ' says Mass every Sunday at the Russian Church in London.

Time passed and I was getting no further. Worse than that : the people to whom I applied met me now with a direct refusal : ' For the time being there can be no question of your crossing the frontier.   If you care to wait—in two or three weeks, circumstances may have altered. . . .'

Two or three weeks ! With Pierre in prison ! When every moment a fresh outbreak of terrorism could be expected ! . . . Two or three weeks when every hour was precious ! Whatever the obstacles, I must not fail him at such a moment !

I decided to see General Youdenich, commander-in-chief of the ' North-Western Army '.   The General received me with great civility, listened to my request, and promised to do ' everything in his power '.   Would he really do it ? I wondered, or was it just the usual polite and meaningless sentence, the unvarying sedative for all ladies in distress ? A short time later I was given to understand that it would be useless to hope for any practical results : the frontier was closed, no one was allowed to pass, etc.   The General's polite promises had made me lose several days.

One evening in the hotel lobby I met Lili Demi-doff. I had known Lili all my life and was agreeably surprised at suddenly coming across her in Hel-singfors. 'What are *you* doing here?' Lili was in the same state of anxiety as myself; her sister Vera had remained in Russia, and for many months now the family had been without news. Lili was haunted by the most sinister forebodings. There was no way of reasoning with her—her fears were not founded on reason. 'But look here, Lili. You know very well that your apprehensions have no grounds. Pierre, as a man, runs a far greater risk than Vera. Moreover, we know Pierre is in prison, and haven't you yourself just been telling me not to lose hope?' It was all in vain. In some mysterious way she knew. . . .

Several months later I heard of the way Vera died, brutally murdered by the Bolsheviks for her refusal to disclose the whereabouts of her husband. They say she was tortured first. . . . In a most hideous way. . . .

Lili offered to accompany me to General Manner-heim, the Dictator of Finland, whose word there was law. Lili had known him ever since those far-off days when he, a smart young guardsman, and she, a blushing *débutante*, had danced together in the fashionable ball-rooms of Petrograd.

Once again I was full of optimism, for there seemed no possible reason why the Dictator should deny me so trifling a service as to help me to penetrate into Russia. The General was most sympathetic, granted us a lengthy interview, and promised to look carefully into the question. My spirits rose accordingly. I was nearly happy. Alas ! a short-lived happiness. The answer received a few days later was quite definite : at present no one was allowed to pass the frontier ; maybe in a few weeks. . . . If I cared to wait. . . .

Always the same old story.

What was I to do ? Waiting was naturally out of the question. But where was help to be found, now that even the Dictator had failed me ?

I could see only one way out of the difficulty : somehow, by fair means or foul, to get as near the frontier as possible, and there find a peasant whom I could bribe to lead me across. Even this was not so simple ; martial law had been proclaimed over the whole district, and no one was admitted within a certain area without a special permit. So the first thing to do was to obtain a permit.

The town of Helsingfors, which had impressed me so favourably at first, with its gaiety and cleanliness, was little by little losing in my eyes a great deal of its charm. The Finns are a hardworking and steadfast people, although of a somewhat heavy and mirthless disposition. At that time their pride in their newly-acquired independence found its chief expression in unrestricted animosity towards

their former rulers.   All those who had a grudge
against Russia gave full vent to their old feelings of
resentment ; others followed their lead and made
us pay, now that we were vanquished, for all the
offences, all the slights they had ever suffered in
the course of history.   At every step we met with
difficulties, petty vexations and delays, humiliating
pin-pricks, and often more than pin-pricks.   We
Russians were as yet unaccustomed to our new
position as ' the pariahs of Europe ', and reacted
painfully to every slur on our national pride.   Just
a question of habit.[1]

(I hope my Finnish friends will forgive me—my
charming and hospitable Finnish friends, whose
kindness helped me through many a black hour.
What would I have done without them !   And,

[1] To those who should suspect me of exaggeration I recommend the
few pages on Finland in Professor Dillon's book *Russia To-day and
Yesterday* (Dent, 1929) : ' I had been away from Helsingfors since the
month of June 1914,' writes Dillon, ' when a large percentage of the
population spoke Russian fluently.   A still larger bi-lingual percentage
was to be found in Viborg and the country along the Russian frontier.
To-day the bi-lingual element—excluding those who speak Swedish—
has vanished.   Nobody speaks or is supposed to understand Russian,
not even those who knew it so thoroughly fourteen years ago.   I tempted
some to bring out their latent knowledge, but they ignored my luring
efforts and resorted to the language of signs.   Once in a while my per-
severance was rewarded with an answer in racy Russian but it was
preceded with a request that I would not reveal this philological back-
sliding to any one.   " Is it an offence then ? " I queried.   " No.   There's
no law against speaking Russian, but all the same, it's unlucky.   Those
who do it, repent." '   These lines were written more than ten years
after the proclamation of Finland's independence.   If this is the feeling
reigning in the country to-day, what must it have been ten years ago,
before the healing hand of time had been able to tune it down to its
present degree of vindictive fierceness ?

incidentally, what would we all have done had the Finnish Government chosen to shut its doors against us, as it could so easily have done at the time? Instead of making spiteful remarks I ought to express to the Finns my gratitude for all the hospitality they gave us.)

The contrast between our situation and that of our former European allies caused us, I must confess, a great deal of envious suffering. We met them everywhere—so very superior, so smart, so lavishly rich, so proud of themselves ; *they* of course found all doors open and met with nothing but smiles and compliments. Masters of the situation, they had no intention of hiding it. Why should they ? Most readers probably remember the story learnt at school of the conqueror who threw his heavy sword into the scales against the ransom of gold and exclaimed : ' *Vae Victis !* ' (' Woe to the vanquished '). A most instructive story.

I was beginning to feel at a loss. Who does not know the hideous nightmare feeling of running at full speed, expending all one's strength, and yet never advancing an inch ? All my efforts, all my endeavours were leading to naught. There was something I could not understand : some invisible wall seemed to stand in my way, some devilish force to obstruct my passage. I was losing patience, hurrying frantically from department to department, applying to one official after another, talking, arguing. . . . All in vain.

One evening the hotel porter rang me up to say that a Russian officer wanted to see me. His name conveyed nothing to me. ' Show him up.' A few minutes later came a knock at the door. ' You do not know me,' began my visitor, ' but I am a friend of your cousin Count Pavlik Schouvaloff. It is only for his sake that I have come to you ; it is contrary to my duty as an officer and in violation of official secrets. I have come to warn you. You have the intention of going to Russia ; you may be quite sure you will never get there. And it is not the Bolsheviks who are going to prevent you. I know for certain that the British Intelligence Service at Helsingfors has received information that you are a Bolshevik agent, carrying a letter to Trotsky. Do not ask where the information came from. I do not know, but even if I did I would not have the right to tell you. Personally, I have no doubt the report is false—otherwise I would not be here. You had better give up all thought of going to Russia, at least for the present. If, nevertheless, you persist in your effort, you will either be arrested or shot down at the frontier. . . .'

That was all he would tell me. The unexpectedness of the blow dazed me ; I stood there, gazing at him, incapable even of formulating a question, and scarcely able to murmur broken thanks as he hurriedly took his leave. On the threshold my visitor turned round. ' If by any chance you are in possession of some incriminating documents, I would strongly advise you to get rid of them at once.'

That was all. Quietly the door closed behind him.

What were the feelings of the old lady who having fallen into a lethargic sleep awoke one day in a closed coffin on her way to the cemetery ? Or those of the famous banker Löwenstein during the few seconds when, having opened the wrong door of his aeroplane, he suddenly realized that his foot was stepping not on to the solid floor of his dressing-room, but into the endless void over the Channel ? Or those of the nameless martyrs in the trenches, who by the criminal mistake of some careless observer unexpectedly found themselves under the deadly barrage of their own artillery ? What did they feel ? Astonishment, pain, indignation, despair ?

I saw at once that, however ridiculous my situation, it would take me endless time and trouble to clear myself. The main issue, and at the same time the chief difficulty, was the need of swift action. Time meant more than money to me, infinitely more, for the liberty, possibly even the life, of Pierre was at stake.

I could of course create a great stir, give vent to my hurt feelings, proclaim my indignation, argue, deny. . . . But I knew that such a course would be both useless and unwise. Affairs of this kind must

be settled behind the scenes. By bringing the case
to light I would start people talking and only harm
myself. The best plan would be to find some
friend who knew me well enough to vouch for my
character, and who at the same time could convince
those in authority. But I was passing through one
of those unlucky periods of life when every single
thing is sure to go wrong. So of course none of
my influential friends happened to be in Finland.
In Stockholm I could, no doubt, easily find such a
person. But that meant delay ; and time was the
only thing that I could not afford to lose.

I would have given a great deal to discover the
origin of this slanderous report. I was utterly at
sea ; I knew of no enemy in the world, and could
hardly admit the idea of any one deliberately trying
to harm me. Or was it all due to some absurd
mistake, some unforeseen coincidence, some fantastic
misunderstanding ? But how ? . . . Why ? . . .

The longer I meditated the harder grew the
problem. I felt sure that the whole infernal business
was connected in some mysterious way with the
letter Eses had given me for Krassin. I was most
unwilling to part with a document that might prove
of the greatest value to me later on in Russia. But
—safety first. So I locked the door and deliberately
burnt the precious paper.

I felt like a rabbit caught in a snare ; like
Carpentier in the ring against Dempsey a few
seconds before the knock-out. Was I to admit

myself beaten, go away and start the whole thing over again from the beginning ? Or was I to make my way on to Petrograd, come what may, ignoring as far as possible both the ' Reds ' and the ' Whites ' ?

My mind was in a turmoil ; the maddest ideas, the most desperate plans raced feverishly through my brain. All the long-forgotten rumours I had ever heard about the horrors of the Tcheka—terrible stories that had been lying dormant in some dark corner of my subconscious mind—now came drifting to the surface. While I lingered here in a state of forced inactivity Pierre was being tortured in some obscure cellar of the Loubianka, was being put slowly to death by yellow-faced Chinese executioners. My imagination conceived gruesome pictures of naked human bodies writhing in agony on the black, slimy floor mottled with patches of slowly-congealing blood. I heard a familiar voice crying out in pain, gazed into a pair of grey eyes darkened by the shadow of death . . . and neither reason nor will-power could end this orgy of shattered nerves, broken suddenly out of all control.

I paced up and down my tiny room, from one corner to the other ; I remained long hours stretched on the bed, smothering my sobs in the pillow in a paroxysm of acute misery. . . . I smoked cigarette after cigarette until I was sick and giddy, until dull stupor took the place of pain. . . .

There were days which I spent in church, on my knees before the miracle-working image of the

Virgin. Nights I passed wandering about the streets, or sitting forlornly on some public bench, until the inquisitive glances of a policeman, or the unwelcome advances of a stray reveller forced me on. Towards morning I would return to the hotel, slip up to my room, and throw myself in utter exhaustion on to the bed, unable any longer to keep back my tears, bitter tears of impotence, rage, and longing.

It is darkest before the dawn. . . . Quite unexpectedly for me Abeecee arrived in Helsingfors. Abeecee—a member of the Intelligence Service, whose work brought him into constant touch with the British M.I.; had I been given the choice I could have asked for no better *deus ex machina* than Abeecee.

' Sandik, Sandik, if you only knew how happy I am to see you ! '

Abeecee went straight to the head of the British Intelligence Service in Finland :

' Is it true that you have been cautioned against Princess Wolkonsky ? ' They consulted their dossiers.

' Yes. She is suspected of being a Bolshevist agent. Information received from you.'

All was explained. The origin of the whole mischief lay in the letter to my husband which I had entrusted to V.—Abeecee's friend in London. The letter had been read, opened by this same

officer who had taken charge of it. On learning
from its contents that I was carrying a letter to
' L. B.', he mistook me for a spy of Trotsky's
(probably under the erroneous impression that L. B.
meant Leon Bronstein [1]), and hurried to the British
authorities : ' Catch the spy.' Sheer stupidity in
the service of a false sense of duty ? Distorted
patriotism combined with a lack of critical reasoning,
based on the usual war spy-mania ? . . .

All's well that ends well. However, my dear V.,
some things are not easily forgotten.

The whole absurd misunderstanding having been
cleared up, there seemed little doubt that my goal
would soon be reached. Abeecee himself had
promised to help me ; and nobody was in a better
position to do so. In a fortnight, at the most, I
would be in Petrograd.

Why did not this happen ? What prevented me ?
Why did our plans all miscarry ? Why should the
messenger we awaited be late, and the person we
needed be away ? One delay after another. A
great deal must be ascribed to bad luck, but part of
the fault was our own. To take but one example :
Abeecee had devised a plan for getting me into
Russia by means of a fast motor-boat. On a dark
night we would slip past Kronstadt and land somewhere near Oranienbaum ; from there I would have
no great difficulty in reaching Petrograd, while

---

[1] Trotsky's real name is Bronstein.

Abeecee returned with the boat to Finland. The plan appealed to me, and the ten days we had to wait while the boat was being overhauled in the docks of Abo passed quickly enough. In the end, however, nothing came of it. To give the boat a trial we had decided to go by sea from Abo to Helsingfors ; but on the way the engine broke down and we were all nearly drowned. The engine trouble proved to be serious, the repairs demanding three weeks or more. As a new boat was too expensive the plan had to be abandoned. The same ill-luck dogged all our endeavours ; whatever we planned, something always went wrong.

I am sure Abeecee sincerely wished to help me ; and was ready to do all he could to get me across the frontier. In theory. But when it came to arranging the actual details, what could be more natural on his part than a desire to make the whole enterprise as safe as possible ? The more he thought of it, the more he tried to eliminate risk ; with each new project, he demanded an ever greater guarantee of safety. It is clear that the man who thinks of safety while preparing for battle is fore-doomed to failure ; so it is hardly surprising that all our plans came to nothing.

Frankly, I cannot even blame Abeecee. No man in the world would enjoy sending his young cousin alone on a dangerous mission into the heart of the enemy camp. It was up to me to urge him on, to insist on his carrying out our plans. But we all know how great is the temptation to lay our burdens on another's shoulders, to let another fight our battles. Afterwards, there is only oneself to blame.

The summer was at an end and the clear, quiet days of early autumn had taken its place. The evening air on the gulf was soft and transparent, and the pine trees near Helsingfors stood dark and beautiful against the red glow of the setting sun ; later, the frogs would start their endless serenade, and the moon shine in splendid indifference, turning the whole sea into one mass of liquid silver through which our boat would glide softly on its way home-wards, past the black shadows of sleeping villages. . . .

From a letter to my daughter :

> *August 2nd, 1919.*
> *Still from Helsingfors*

Time seems to have stopped. Nothing changes, nothing happens. No news from Petrograd. No possibility of getting there. The only agreeable event these days was the arrival of your two letters from Bath. . . . Am trying to learn Swedish—just for the sake of doing something. It will be one of the many useless things I have done in my life . . .'

Towards the end of August, Abeecee declared that he would have to go to Reval. Reval had by now supplanted Helsingfors as the centre of Russian anti-Bolshevik activities : the headquarters

of Youdenich's Army had been transferred to Reval ;
Reval was also the residence of the newly-born
' North-Western Government '.[1]

It was clearly time for us to go to Reval. I say
' us ' because it never even entered my head to
remain in Helsingfors. All my hopes of crossing
the frontier depended on my cousin's organization ;
relied on his staff, his messengers, etc. His failure
in getting me across the frontier by way of Finland
only made it the more important that we should
succeed by way of Esthonia. There was no more
time to lose.

A few days before leaving Helsingfors I called on
Professor N., my former teacher and one of the
ablest surgeons in Russia ; also one of the noblest
and purest men on earth.

[1] Few Englishmen know the story of the latter's formation ; nor how
General Marsh, head of the British Military Mission, having assembled
certain Russians in the British Consulate at Reval, on the 10th of August
1919, presented them with an ultimatum, to constitute immediately,
without leaving the room, a new Russian Government, whose first
act would be the recognition of the Sovereign State of Esthonia (formerly
one of the Baltic provinces of Russia), and the signing of a treaty with
her. If in half an hour the new Government was not yet formed,
England, according to General Marsh, would refuse all further support
to the White Army. So saying, General Marsh left the room, at 6.40
p.m. precisely. When he re-entered it at 7 p.m. the North-Western
Government had been formed, the ministers chosen according to the
list provided by General Marsh. The docility of the Russians is to a
certain degree explained by the recent arrival of two British steamers in
Reval, with guns, ammunition, and tanks for the Youdenich Army ;
and the knowledge that two more steamers were on the way. The
threatened withdrawal of all further co-operation on the part of the
Allies, meant an immediate collapse of the Army and the abandonment
of all hope of a successful march on Petrograd. Anything was better than
that.—(See *Archives of the Russian Revolution*, Vol. I, edited in Russian
by I. Hessen in Berlin).

'Professor, I am going to Russia. Mine is a dangerous errand—if I am caught I will most certainly be treated as a spy. You know what that means, and you also know what women have had to endure at the hands of the Red soldiers. A swift, clean death is to be prayed for. I need something handier, easier to conceal than a revolver. Will you help me?'

A long silence followed. He was sitting at the table, his eyes fixed on the open window, a faraway, dreamy expression on his face. He never even looked at me, seemed to have forgotten my very existence. Another few seconds passed. Silence. Had I come to the wrong man, I wondered. . . .

'What is it you want?'

'Well, I think a dose of morphia would be the simplest; also the easiest to obtain.'

'You are right.'

He took a sheet of paper and began writing.

'How much do you need?'

'I leave that to you, Professor.'

Was it my imagination, or did the pen really tremble slightly in his fingers as he signed his name at the end of the prescription.

'There.'

'Thank you, Professor.'

A curious thing is the human language: the same word 'thank you' in a case like this, and in answer to the polite gesture of a neighbour passing you the salt.

A few insignificant sentences, then I took my leave. We have not met since. I sometimes wonder whether he remembers me. For my part, the name of Professor N. is among those which no amnesia can ever wipe out of my mind.

The quiet old town of Reval was in a state of feverish excitement; never in all its history had it been the centre of so many varied activities. Here were head-quarters both of the North-Western and Esthonian Armies, here also were the seats of both Governments—the newly-formed Russian one and the scarcely much older Esthonian; here were the numerous foreign missions, the intelligence officers, agents and representatives of all nationalities, and shady characters of no nationality at all. . . . All hotels were full, all furnished rooms had been let. The coffee-houses were overcrowded, the restaurants and night-clubs open till the small hours of the morning, with music playing, wine flowing, and noisy quarrels adding to the general excitement. Those were lively days for the small provincial town of Reval, suddenly, by a whim of fate, promoted to the rank of capital of an independent State and a focus of interest for the whole of Europe.

After a long search all through the town we secured two small rooms near Ekaterinenthal. Small but clean ones, in the house of a neat old lady, just outside the town; we could not have hoped for better. There was no bathroom in the house,

3

no central heating, no running water in the rooms, etc. ; however, these were but minor inconveniences. We had not come to Reval in search of comfort.

Our first visit was to M. Staroselsky, Abeecee's agènt in Reval, who, according to Abeecee, would be able to arrange my passage over the frontier. Staroselsky was a brisk little man, with black hair and clever, shifty little eyes. I think he disliked me from the first. He disliked my presence in Reval, disliked my friendship with Abeecee. He probably ascribed Abeecee's prolonged stay in the Baltic to his desire to help me out of my trouble. He considered it high time Abeecee went back to London and abandoned me to my fate, whatever that might be. He thought—but I really have no right to speak of his thoughts ; he never confided in me, and outwardly his manners were always as charming and as polite as could be desired. As to Abeecee—well, no doubt he did want to help me. But, whatever any one says, we all know Abeecee is certainly not a man to put private interests before the requirements of duty. If he stayed in Esthonia he probably did so as he knew that things were shortly going to happen up there. And events soon proved him to be right.

Days passed, and still nothing changed ; it was the same as at Helsingfors. Again the messenger we expected from Russia failed to turn up ; then rumours reached us of disorders along the frontier

—better wait a few days till things calm down ; and so on and so forth.

I was living from day to day in the certainty that if not this week, then the next, I would be sure to start.

It is difficult to say how long this state of expectancy would have lasted if the quiet of our everyday existence had not been suddenly shattered by a series of telegrams from London, urgently demanding the immediate return of Abeecee. I made no effort to keep him back ; not from a sense of duty or unwillingness to hamper his work—oh, no ! It was merely that I knew no words of mine would have the power of retaining him in Reval now that the interests of his work called him away. Abeecee was of course quite positive that his absence would make no difference to me ; Staroselsky would be there to take all necessary steps, and I could rest assured that in ten days at the latest I would be in Russia. It all sounded very logical. But logic was the last thing in the world that I wanted. For who ever heard of logic calming the anxiety of a nervous woman, or of sound reasoning helping anybody to feel less miserable ! Abeecee was my chief support, psychologically as well as practically. On his departure the ground seemed to slip from under my feet.

Oh, those long, dreary days ! Nothing to do but to wait. Nothing to read, all books having been read and re-read ages ago. Not even a good,

not even a bad detective story ; not a single Phillips
Oppenheim nor an Edgar Wallace.   Misery !

I spent a week-end with my brother-in-law
and his children at Schloss Fall, the famous residence of the Wolkonsky family. Lovely Fall,
with its once beautiful old house, its big park
running down to the seashore, and the waterfall
with a number of quaint little bridges thrown over
the stream.

The storm of war and revolution had passed over
Fall. When I first entered the house, I caught my
breath at the appalling sight : the floors in all the
rooms were littered with the debris of broken
furniture, with shreds of silk torn down from the
chairs, with bits of glass, broken china, old porcelain
statuettes smashed to pieces and scattered about.
The grand piano, relic of days long passed, stood
with its keys battered in, its legs broken, reclining
heavily against the wall ; its polished surface like
the back of some huge animal, kneeling silently in
the agony of mortal wounds. And covering all lay
a thick white carpet of leaves torn out of books,
hundreds upon hundreds of printed sheets—all that
was left of the rare old books in French, English,
German, and Russian whose costly bindings had
been thrown in an untidy heap in one of the corners.
Many a letter, kept with love and care, treasured
from generation to generation, lay torn and crumpled
on the dusty floor, viciously trampled on by the
heavy, dirty boots of the invaders. A well-known

RIVER SIDE

COURT SIDE

FALL, THE COUNTRY HOUSE OF THE WOLKONSKY FAMILY IN ESTHONIA

handwriting caught my eye.   Yes, of course, I would
have recognized it among a thousand : a letter of
Pierre to his mother.   For the first time in our
married life I felt glad Pierre was not with me.   For
him, with his knowledge of the past, his devotion
to family heirlooms, his nearly Oriental veneration
of his ancestors, his love of the house where he had
grown up, and where his father and grandfather
had lived before him—the sight would have been
too much.

Never before had I realized the intensity of hatred
of which human beings are capable.   It was the
wantonness of the destruction, the sheer stupidity
of it, that hurt most.   Had they robbed the house,
taken whatever they wanted, or divided the spoils,
it would not have mattered so much.   But this was
different.   Here was destruction for its own sake :
the low envious hate of the brute for everything
above him, the desire to tear down, trample into
mud all that was noble and beautiful.   Here were
the lowest instincts of the human animal let loose—
let loose against us and all we stood for in life :
culture, order, tradition, cleanliness, honour.   Had
we been on the spot they would have probably torn
our limbs with the same ferocity with which they
had torn to bits the books of the library ; they would
have smashed our skulls with even greater pleasure
than they had smashed the eighteenth-century
Sèvres statuettes.

Casting one last look round I hurried away from

the tragic scene—one last look to see if by any chance something had escaped destruction. No, not one book untorn, not one unbroken chair. . . . Only one thing remained unharmed in the whole house : an enormous vase of black jasper, the size of a man—a splendid gift of Tsar Nicholas I to Pierre's great-grandfather. It had been thrown down, overturned, its rim bore the mark of an axe ; but all had been in vain, the vase remained intact. One can imagine the fury of that horde of vandals when in their orgy of senseless annihilation they suddenly came against this thing of beauty that all their efforts were unable to destroy. Thrown down, gashed, beaten—the black stone of the Tsar remained unimpaired. What a symbol !

I could easily have accepted my brother-in-law's invitation to stay with them a few days longer were it not for the feverish restlessness that took hold of me as soon as I left the town. I had hardly travelled a few miles before the idea began to torment me that something had happened in Reval—something of the greatest importance which would make me miss the chance I had been expecting for months. So I hurried back to town, working myself up into a state of quite unfounded excitement, only to find that nothing at all had taken place, and that the date of my departure was as uncertain as ever. And once more the long, dreary days dragged on.

There are times in life when loneliness is more

THE JASPER VASE

THE DISORDER AFTER THE RAID

FALL

than one can bear, when a few kind words, an insignificant friendly gesture, will preserve one from a whole night of nervous insomnia. It was a great comfort to know that I could always knock at the door of the Zinovieffs, that there would always be a welcome cup of tea, and the possibility of whiling away some particularly long afternoon. At times I would pay a visit to Mrs. Volmer-Hansen, wife of the representative of the Danish Red Cross ; on Sunday afternoons her house was the rendezvous of British naval officers and vague foreigners of all nationalities, who danced the latest fox-trot to the tune of a gramophone record. Mrs. Volmer-Hansen did me one great service : she showed me how to darn stockings. It seems ridiculous that I should have lived to be over thirty without the smallest idea of the method by which this was accomplished. ' Better late than never. . . .' In this case, frankly, I would have much preferred it to have been ' never '.

But my chief, my only important occupation was a daily visit to Staroselsky. ' Why trouble to come all the way here, Princess ? ' he would say politely. ' I will send you word as soon as the messenger due from Petrograd has arrived. I can't imagine what is keeping him so long.' Staroselsky was as anxious as I for the arrival of the messenger who was to bring him news from his wife—his young wife and two-year-old baby who were staying with her parents somewhere near Petrograd. The sword of

Damocles hung over their heads; should the
Bolsheviks recognize in them the family of a 'White'
officer the thread would inevitably snap. No wonder
his nerves were in no better state than mine.

The ten days' limit fixed by Abeecee for my
departure had passed. A day—two—five days
more. Nothing happened. How long was I going
to wait?

I knew that Abeecee had been obliged to interrupt
his journey and was actually in Stockholm. I went
to the post office, took out a telegram form and
wrote:

No further developments Stop Please come back need
you badly . . .

Four days later Abeecee was in Reval.

From that moment events began to move. One
dark night, in pouring rain, Staroselsky and I
cautiously crept through the labyrinth of crooked,
narrow streets of the old town. Our goal was a
smelly little room behind a cobbler's shop, where
in exchange for a large sum of money I was handed
an authentic member's ticket of the Esthonian
Communist Party. How could honest people ever
manage without the help of traitors? There was
nothing extraordinary in his face—the usual face
of a skilled workman, with no stamp of ignominy
on it, none of the usual features of the traitor of

'CROOKED, NARROW STREETS OF THE OLD TOWN'
IN REVAL

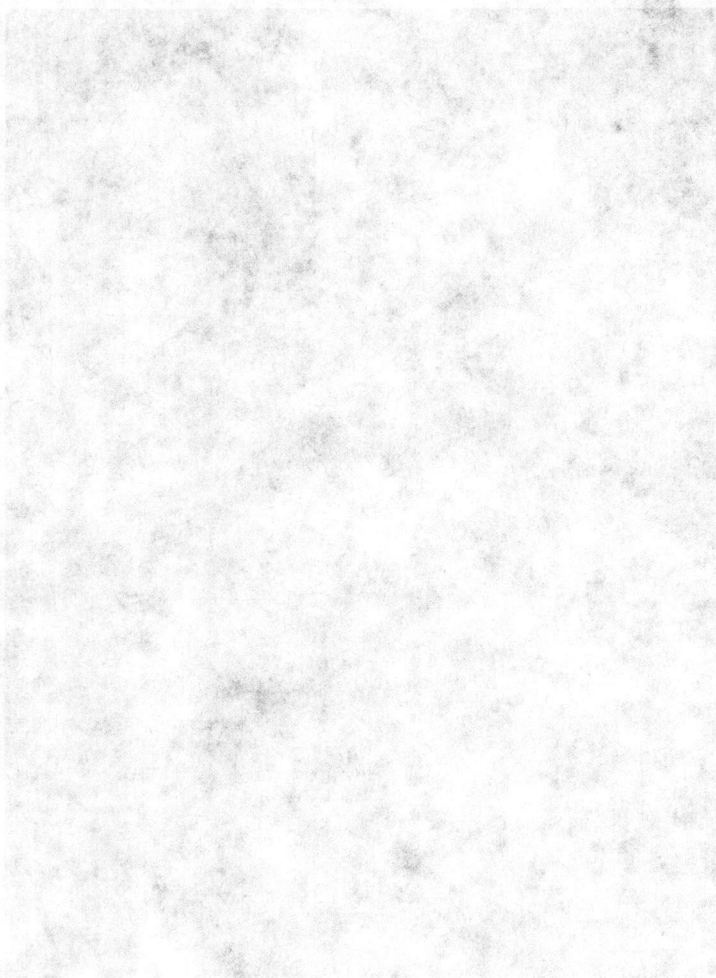

detective fiction about him. (In this case life had not yet imitated art.)

With the document just bought I would at least be protected against immediate arrest on crossing the Russian frontier. The day and hour of my departure were next decided upon. After that our conference was at an end.

We returned in the same silent way in which we had come ; we had to be sure of not being followed. When I reached home I was wet to the skin, trembling as much from cold as from excitement and anticipated fear. The plan we had elaborated seemed to me unsatisfactory in many ways : on a moonless night, at the beginning of next week, I would be taken across the Peipus Lake and set down on the opposite bank, on Russian territory. Under the assumed character of an Esthonian Communist I was then to find my way to Pskov and deliver a letter to one of the Bolshevik leaders of the town. (The letter as well as my member's ticket were quite authentic, coming straight from the Communist head-quarters in Reval.) Later, then, it would be up to me to arrange for my passage to Petrograd. But although I had been given some instructions, I felt the whole plan was extremely perilous. I am a poor liar, have always despised that weapon of cowards. Not that the moral aspect of it troubled me now. I was ready to stoop to any lies, use any weapon, down to the foulest, in my fight for Pierre's safety. But I sensed that the part I was about to play was full of pitfalls, and had no doubt that the smallest mistake would land me in the hands of the Tcheka. However, there was no choice. The idea of any further delay was simply unbearable. In four days I was going to start.

Many years later, in Paris, I asked Abeecee one day : 'Tell me, Sandik, how is it that, after all those weeks and weeks of deliberation, you chose me such an extremely dangerous and disagreeable way of getting into Russia ?'

Abeecee only smiled. 'You never really went that way, after all.'

No, fate decided otherwise. (Perhaps even then Abeecee knew of what was going to happen ? It is quite possible. And silently enjoyed the sight of my somewhat solemn and in reality perfectly useless preparations ? Also quite possible).

I remember so clearly those last days in Reval, my mood of feverish impatience combined with a sinking sensation in the stomach when I thought of what lay before me ; my long, lonely walks along the paths of the big, silent park, the rustle of dead leaves underfoot ; the clear cold morning air, the smell of the sea, the distant towers of the quaint old city, and through it all, making my pulse race and my hands tremble, the hope that soon, very soon, I would see Pierre.

REVAL

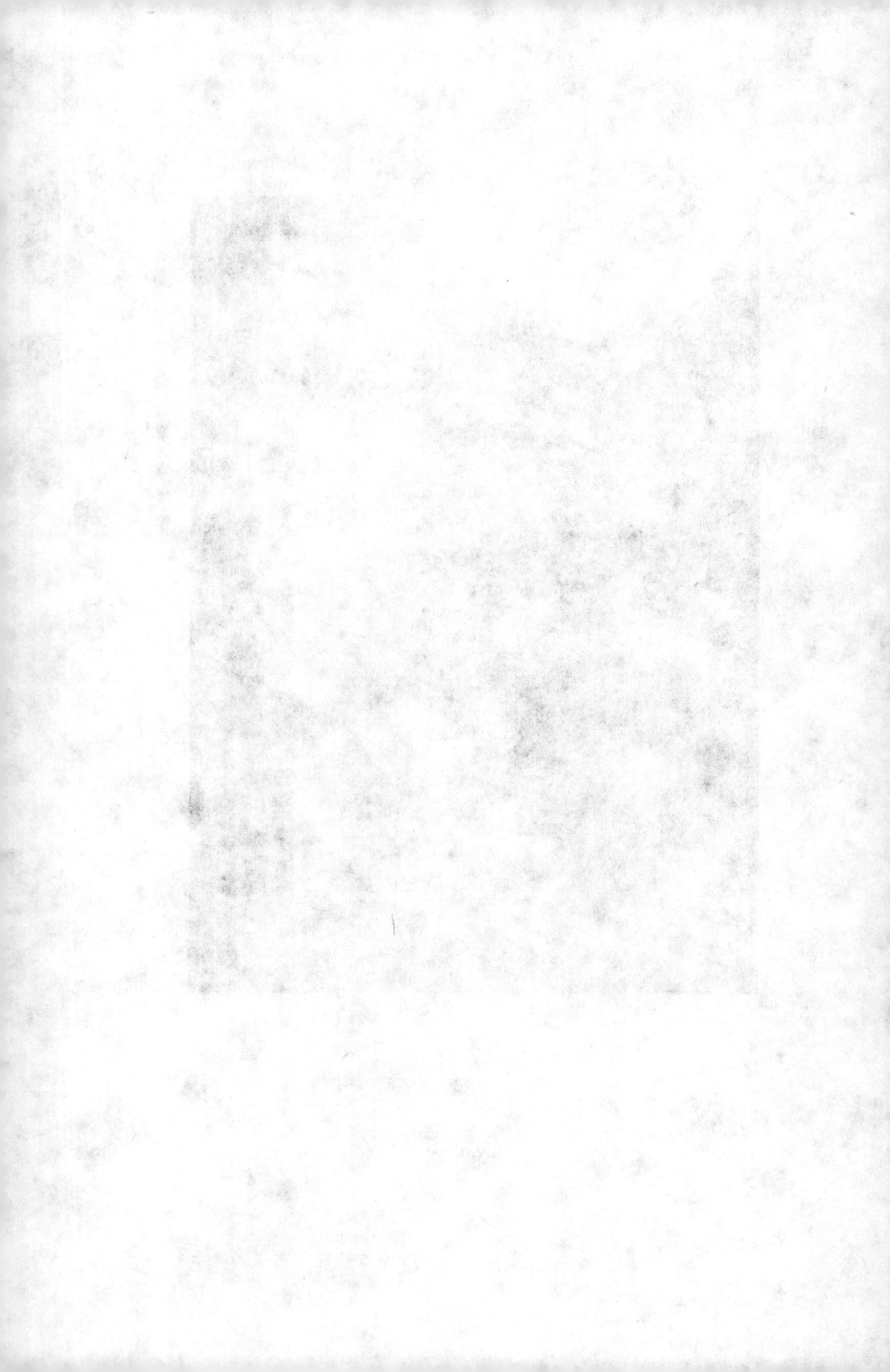

The date of my departure was fixed for Tuesday night. And on Sunday, the first rumours reached us of an advance by the White Army on Petrograd.

Next day the news was officially confirmed : our troops were rapidly advancing towards the capital ; the Bolsheviks were fleeing panic-stricken. How describe our enthusiasm ? We had not the least doubt concerning the issue : in a day or two Petrograd would be taken ; the nightmare of Bolshevism would be ended, a new life was going to begin. There may have been a few sober voices ; we never heeded them. I remember the indignation with which we met the cautious warning of Mrs. Volmer-Hansen : ' You had better delay your rejoicing until Petrograd is taken.' What could she, a foreigner, understand of Russian psychology ! How could we doubt ? We knew instinctively that the turning-point had at last been reached, that the Russian people had awakened, had shaken off their proverbial placidity, and that now the hours of Communism were numbered. The only thing that marred my happiness was the thought of the acts of cruelty the Bolsheviks were sure to commit at the last moment : Trotsky's famous threat of ' banging the door behind him '. As far as possible I tried to forget it.

My plan of going into Russia by way of Pskov was naturally cancelled ; it was clearly both simpler and safer for me to follow the advancing army.

My one fear was to be late for the entry of the
troops into the capital. (And God forbid that Pierre
should have been transferred elsewhere !)

All necessary arrangements were soon finished ;
in my state of excitement I would let no one rest
until I had obtained all required documents, permits,
etc. The train only went as far as Narva. A small
provincial town, just behind the lines, it presented
the usual aspect of war-time chaos ; the streets
were crowded with soldiers, nurses in uniform,
hospital orderlies, etc. ; the usual Red Cross lorries
and artillery guns stood blocking the way and
impeding the whole traffic ; the air was full of
shouting, quarrelling, disorder : even more shouting,
more disorder than one would have expected. . . .
Oh, well, let us not start criticizing already ! Let
us try and get on, one way or another, without
losing time. On . . . on. . . .

Luck was with us. Count A. Ignatieff, of the
International Red Cross, kindly offered us places in
the big motor-lorry that was conveying him with a
load of Red Cross stores to Gatchina. We were
not the only passengers, as besides Abeecee and
myself there were also the young Count Nieroth,
Ignatieff's secretary, my cousin Lulik Meyendorff,
and a few others. In different circumstances it
would have been a charming party. But a person
obsessed by a fixed idea makes a poor travelling
companion.

The big, heavy lorry crawled on slowly, terribly

slowly; the motor roared and the whole car shook, nearly throwing us off our seats at every bump on the battered road. My impatience grew with every minute; what if our troops had already entered Petrograd? My whole being was yearning to be there, with them, at the great moment. . . . The slowness of our clumsy vehicle was exasperating! My pulse seemed to beat in unison with the throbbing of the engine. If only the muscles of my heart had been allowed to drive the pistons up and down the cylinders—God, how we should have flown!

That night we stopped at Yambourg. Such is the name of the spot where Fate chose to play me the most maddening practical joke that ever fell to my lot.

We had, all of us, naturally taken only the minimum of luggage. I had two things with me: one was a bag containing all my personal belongings— some linen, a few toilet things, my new fountain-pen, a small electric torch, the bottle of Guerlain scent Eses had brought me from Paris, etc.—every object chosen with the greatest care and deliberation, as though for an expedition to the South Pole with Colonel Byrd. Many months would possibly elapse before I once more found myself in civilized surroundings. The second thing I had taken with me was the box of dry stores from Fortnum & Mason's, which I had defended tooth and nail against the customs officers of many frontiers : Swedish, Finnish, Esthonian. . . . I would probably have let it go long ago were it not for the picture that so vividly teased my imagination : Pierre in prison, after weeks and weeks of Soviet diet, enjoying oatmeal biscuits, chocolate, sardines, and a glass of old brandy. It was worth a great deal of discomfort. However, the sad story of my box is still to come.

It was beginning to get dark when we reached Yambourg. Thanks to the energy of Ignatieff, a shelter for the night was soon found—no easy matter in a small town where every corner was occupied by soldiers. Our accommodation for the night was far from comfortable, but a well-heated room was something in itself. In that part of the world October nights are often exceedingly cold ; and the month was drawing to its close. The lorry with all the things in it was parked in a military enclosure.

All those who have been through the war remember how the most ordinary everyday things had a way of suddenly becoming almost unattainable luxuries. In that God-forsaken spot it was no small effort to procure even a cup of tea. We were all tired, hungry, and low-spirited when at last supper of a sort was laid on the table. Suddenly I started worrying about my bag that had remained on the lorry with the rest of the luggage. What if somebody were to steal it during the night ? What a calamity !

As bad luck would have it, one of our party
announced his intention of fetching something from
the lorry.   I at once asked Abeecee to go with him
and bring me my bag ; otherwise, I assured him,
I would never be able to close my eyes for a minute.
Abeecee complied with my wishes. Night had
meanwhile settled down ; outside it was pitch dark.
Silently we sat round the table, waiting for the
return of our friends. The minutes passed slowly.
What could they be doing all that time ?   At last
we heard the street-door bang. One look at
Abeecee's face was enough to tell me that something
had gone wrong. His hands were empty. And
my bag ? . . . Yes, I had guessed—the bag had
vanished. Having taken it off the lorry and deposited
it on the ground nearby, Abeecee turned aside to
say a few words to a friend. When he looked round
the bag was not there. The night was dark, soldiers
were constantly passing up and down the road,
nobody had seen anything. Where could one look
for the thief ? After a vain search Abeecee had to
give it up.

At once we sat down to write a complaint to the
military commander, to the chief of the garrison, to
the local police, but all the time we knew it was
hopeless. The whole North-Western Army was
on its way through Yambourg ; the officials had
other things to worry about, matters more important
than the disappearance of a lady's bag. Naturally.
But that did not make it any easier for me. What

was I to do ?   I was left without anything, without even a change of linen or a piece of soap.   Neither at Yambourg nor at Gatchina would I be able to buy anything.   Even in Petrograd it would be difficult, those being the early honeymoon months of Communism, when in strict obedience to theory all shops had been closed and all commerce prohibited.   To go back to Reval ?   No, that was out of the question. Let my last shirt be taken from my back, I would go to Petrograd.

Angrily I glared at Abeecee, who sat in silence, an expression of deep suffering on his face.

You are miserable ?   Do you imagine I am happy ?

Early next morning we continued our way to Gatchina.

I have no intention of describing the general political situation ; nor the feelings of the population towards the advancing White Army.   I've been told that in several villages imposing ceremonies of welcome took place.   Maybe.   We came too late to witness anything of the kind.   Our own contact with the inhabitants was of the slightest, being limited to rare occasions, such as a burst tyre or the need of a pail of water for the radiator.   My general impression was that the people were on their guard, cautious not to commit themselves definitely.   In the towns, what interested them most was to know whether we were bringing supplies.

I am in no position to pass comment upon the

reasons that led to the defeat of the Whites.   They
were probably many ;   among others, our failure
to reach an agreement with Finland, the fact that
the British Fleet refused us help at the most critical
moment. . . . There may have been a thousand
others.   What do I know !   A great deal lay probably in the lowering of the moral standard among
the troops ;   we were far from being an army of
unsullied knighthood.   It is no use denying it now.

As far as I can judge, one of the chief mistakes of
the White Staff lay in its inability to procure enough
supplies for the conquered provinces.   Those who
went hungry under the Reds continued to do so
under the Whites.   So why trouble helping one
side in preference to the other ?   A few trains of
white flour distributed at the right moment might
possibly have changed the issue of the whole cam-
paign. . . . But what's the use of crying over
spilt milk ?

The first thing on reaching Gatchina was to look
for some temporary abode.   There could be no
question of an hotel ;   several months of Bolshevik
régime would have seen to that.   However, we—
Ignatieff, Nieroth, Abeecee and I—were lucky enough
to find rooms with a former landlady of mine ;   two
years ago I had passed a whole summer in Gatchina,
as pupil of the Military School of Aviation—one of
the happiest periods of my life.   Every flyer knows
the splendour of those morning flights, the nervous

4

tension of the beginner, the feeling of joy and peace alone above the clouds, then the first rays of the rising sun and the long gliding descent down, down on to the earth. . . .

That was two years ago. Quite a good many things can happen in two years !

Having tidied up a bit (and shed a few more tears over my missing bag), we started out for head-quarters, impatient to learn about the happenings of the last twenty-four hours. Also, both Abeecee and Ignatieff had some serious questions to discuss with the commanding officer.

Rodzianko was there and ready to receive us.

'What about Petrograd ? Will it be for to-morrow ? '

' Well, well, hardly as soon as that.'

There followed a few explanations which struck us as rather vague. We had been expecting something very different. However . . .

As soon as possible I put in my question :

' And how's Pavlik Schouvaloff ? '

I had been told his regiment was somewhere near Gatchina. The answer was slow in coming.

' You've not heard ? '

' No, what is it ? Wounded ? Dead ? '

Rodzianko looked away.

' Yesterday morning, not far from here. He was hit in the side by a bit of shrapnel. Died in hospital a few hours later.'

The first conscious reaction is one of incredulity : it cannot be, there must have been a mistake somewhere. . . .

Do other people's brains work in the same way, I wonder ? In those first moments do their minds also refuse to grasp the appalling news, just passing it by as so many senseless words. And then, after seconds of numbness, somewhere deep down inside, like a sudden spasm of pain, the piercing realization : you will never see him again. Never.

The funeral was next day. How different are the many funerals one has attended in one's life ! Pompous official ceremonies and intimate family gatherings. . . . Funerals in cholera - stricken Macedonia : the big yawning hole, the row of simple wooden boxes lowered hastily into the earth. . . . Later, war funerals at the front, the simple field altar, the modest wooden crosses and the words of the priest drowned by the constant roar of artillery. I thought of one such funeral that I had attended together with Pavlik ; one of our men had been killed during the bombardment. We had been in the same Red Cross Field Unit, Pavlik and I had been together all through the first glorious year of the War. . . . Later, ignoring an old injury in the leg, which had caused him to be discharged from service, he left the Red Cross and enlisted as a volunteer. Not into the Guards, but into an ordinary infantry regiment of Siberian Rifles. Just like him. Our ways parted, and for the next two or three years we hardly met. The last time I saw him was during the winter of 1919, when he came secretly to Petrograd, in order to try and rescue the four grand dukes imprisoned by the Bolsheviks. He arrived too late : all four had just been shot. Two or three days later Pavlik succeeded in crossing the frontier with the Princess Paleï, widow of the murdered Grand Duke Paul. One of his nights at Petrograd, Pavlik spent with us. (I offer it as a case for the moralist : how far has any one the right to shelter a White officer when living under the roof of his old mother, thereby exposing her to the risk of arrest, prison, or even worse ? The decision to do so cost Pierre much moral suffering.)

That was the last time I saw Pavlik—clever, amusing, light-hearted Pavlik. He was, naturally, one of the first to join the White Army : a noble act, a courageous gesture. . . . The End. . . . Why is it always the best that perish ? *Unkraut vergeht nicht.*

It is difficult to specify when we first grasped the fact that things were not going well at the front. It was at the beginning nothing but a vague suspicion, a guilty secret we did not dare to acknowledge even to ourselves. We spoke of a temporary suspension of the advance, only for the time required to bring up reinforcements. We were afraid of looking one another in the face, afraid of reading there the dreaded news we were keeping locked in our hearts. But the day came when concealment was no longer possible. Ominous rumours, leaving their shady hiding-places, spread openly all over the town.   On all faces was written the same expression of helplessness, fear, despair. . . .

In theory I had of course always admitted the possibility of defeat.   My plan of action was ready : I was simply going to remain in Gatchina, and would thus find myself after the retreat of the White Army automatically transferred to the other side.   The best and easiest way of crossing the frontier.

' Under pressure of superior enemy forces, our valiant troops have been obliged to retreat. . . .' Gatchina was going to be abandoned.   The order had already been given. . . . Still I went on hoping : a change of fortune, a battle won, the Red Army in flight. . . .

The evacuation had begun ; long lines of wagons filled the streets.   All those who could left with the army ; it looked as if the whole population of the town were going.   I knew now that there was no more hope left.   The game was up.   Something in me, however, clung desperately to my former illusions : events much more improbable had happened before, miracles were known to have taken place.   Many times. . . . Why not this time ? How gladly would one have given up all the narrow-minded pride of the free-thinker, the materialistic confidence based on years of scientific training—for the sake of one small miracle !

The first of our party to leave were Ignatieff and

Nieroth. ' Kniaginioushka, dearest, do come with us ! You must be mad to contemplate staying behind. Think of the risk ! '

' Impossible. Do not ask me. Risk or no risk, I must stay.'

Abeecee had decided to remain a day or two longer. Like me he was probably hoping for a miracle. Together we went to the station to see the others off. Nothing but blank faces . . . consternation . . . defeat. . . .

For a long time we stood on the platform gazing after the disappearing train, unable to tear ourselves away.

' And we, Sandik, what is going to happen to us ? '

Abeecee was among the last ; head-quarters had left, all those we knew had vanished one after the other.

' Sandik, dear, isn't it time you also went ? '

It must have been the very last train. Nobody could tell us at what hour it would start : some time during the night. We said good-bye at the station. It was bitterly cold. People were hurrying up and down the platform, the whole place was in confusion. A single dull lamp lit up the scene. We both felt utterly miserable. Abeecee was shivering, his face flushed, his hands icy cold. ' Sandik, you are ill ? ' (At the time I hardly realized the gravity of his illness. Only many months after did I learn that on reaching Narva next day he collapsed with some kind of brain fever, and lay for a long time in delirium, oblivious of all around him.)

The tension of waiting became unbearable. We said good-bye, and I returned to my room in the strangely silent, empty house. I lay down on my bed, too exhausted even to undress. Half an hour, an hour went by. . . . Suddenly, a knock at the door. 'Sandik!' . . . Is it possible? A momentary flash of hope: the Communists beaten, the Whites returning.

'No, no, I have only learnt that my train isn't due to leave until two in the morning.'

Silently we sat side by side in the dusk. Words were useless. We were far too unhappy; it hurt us too much to think of the ruin of the White cause.

'Sandik, you've got fever; better go and lie down in the car.'

A few insignificant words, one last handshake. . . . He was gone.

Should we ever see one another again?

CHAPTER III

' Oh le bon temps—J'étais si malheureuse ! '

MY landlady and I were now all alone in the empty house that stood forlornly in its large garden on the outskirts of the town : a frightened half-empty town, silently awaiting it knew not what terrible morrow.

For several days Gatchina remained unoccupied by either Reds or Whites. We lived in ignorance of what was going on around us, cut off from the world, unheeded, forgotten. Rumours strange and vague, improbable and even frankly impossible, flew from house to house, filled the air with a murmur of anxious whisperings : ' Have you heard ? They say the Bolsheviks have burnt down Tsarskoe. The Chinese troops did it. They killed all the men and took the women. Then they set fire to the town and fled. Now they are coming here.'

' God have mercy on us ! ' [1]

Four days passed—four long days and even longer nights. We would wake up in the morning uncertain as to whether the next dawn would see us alive. We prayed for an end to this suspense, but trembled at the thought of the unknown calamities any change was sure to bring us. The atmosphere

---

[1] Needless to say there was no word of truth in the report.

of panic that enveloped the town grew more
and more intense each day, the rumours became
wilder and more contradictory.   One could not dis-
criminate between truth and fiction ; in those days
nothing was impossible ; the strangest fantasies
had turned into facts, life had been changed into a
nightmare.

It must have been about three o'clock in the afternoon that the Red troops entered Gatchina.   I was
returning from the Cathedral, after having put some
fresh flowers on Pavlik's grave, when I caught sight
of them : a Red infantry regiment advancing in full
marching order.   The soldiers looked happy and
good-natured (nothing like victory to keep up the
spirits of the army).   The usual street-urchins ran
alongside the regiment, a dozen or so local Communists stood shouting their welcome.   Some one
next to me explained that this same regiment had
been stationed in Gatchina before the White
advance ; the soldiers recognized old acquaintances
among the crowd, jokes and greetings were ex-
changed.   On a balcony a man stood waving a red
flag.   There was nothing awe-inspiring in this
entry of the Red conquerors into the vanquished
town.   Nothing, it would seem, to justify the terror
in which we had all awaited the event.   Still, the
people I met in the street looked gloomy and pre-
occupied ; fear was clearly written in their eyes.
Of course, it is possible that my own state of mind
may have impaired the accuracy of my observations ;

it is a well-known psychological fact that a person will often project his own mood on to his surroundings, and quite unconsciously attribute his own feelings to others.

I hurried homewards ; it was not safe for me to be out in the streets. There was the risk that some one might recognize me, some one who remembered having seen me in the company of White officers, or even entering divisional head-quarters. Danger might be lurking round every corner ; every innocent-looking passer-by was possibly planning to denounce me. No, decidedly, I could not remain in Gatchina, and the sooner I left the better. In a little town like this each cockroach seems to be known by sight. It would not be long before the usual routine of Bolshevik occupation was started : registration of the inhabitants, searches in the houses, with arrests and executions as their natural sequel. Once the net was drawn they would let no one escape. My only chance lay in immediate action. Besides, it was only in Petrograd that I could obtain news of Pierre.

To get away. Yes. But how ? Easier said than done. The railway trains were not running, and a certain time was sure to elapse before they were once more accessible to the public. And then, special permits, certificates, and so forth would be required ; travelling in Soviet Russia was no simple matter. A casual inquiry, ' Comrade, your papers,' and I would be lost.

To hire a car ?   Out of the question ; one of the first acts of the Communist Government had been to requisition all private cars and shut all private garages.   The glittering Rolls-Royce is what excites most envy in the breast of the destitute.   I am now fully qualified to judge.   It was risky to hire even the simplest vehicle : questions would be asked, thoughts would be awakened in idle brains . . . and in the circumstances, starting a train of thought in another's head would be to set a match to the mine under my feet.   In moments of great danger insects lie quite still, feigning death ; any un-necessary movements may attract the attention of the foe.   For me the best way to pass unnoticed would be to go on foot.

The distance between Gatchina and Petrograd is approximately forty-two versts : [1] A far from agreeable prospect for me who hate walking and have always, when possible, avoided using my legs as a means of locomotion.   However, there seemed to be no choice.   On the morrow I would start.

My last evening in Gatchina.   All preparations were completed ; it was soon time to go to bed.   I sat in the kitchen with my landlady, our meagre supper just finished.   Our nerves were in a bad state. How could we help it ? the Bolsheviks were in the town, any moment they might come and search the house ; perhaps to-night, or to-morrow, or in a month.   Nobody knew.   Anything was possible.

[1] A verst represents two-thirds of a mile.

Mrs. Pousseff's house stood in a lonely place ; were we to call for help, no one would even hear. . . .

' Aren't you afraid of staying here all alone after I have gone ? '

Mrs. Pousseff only shrugged her shoulders. Fatalism ? Faith in the ever-vigilant protective hand of the Deity ? Or miserly unwillingness to part with the few roubles a servant-girl would have cost her ?

Suddenly we heard a strange sound ; it seemed to be coming from within the house. Our rooms were upstairs, the ground floor was shut up and locked. We strained our ears : ' Somebody is walking downstairs,' and Mrs. Pousseff seized the candlestick. I had great difficulty in keeping her from going down to investigate ; it does not always pay to play the hero. I knew we were powerless to deal with the intruders ; our only chance lay in making them think the house was empty ; as they could hardly take away the furniture, they (whoever they were) would probably leave in the same way as they had come. We put out the light and sat down to wait : two badly frightened women listening in the dead of the night to the steps of the burglars . . . Very photogenic.

The heavy footsteps of our uninvited visitors resounded through the house. One could hear them moving from room to room ; then one of them opened the piano and began playing. It was evidently no thief. Raffles himself did not indulge in music while at work. They could only be soldiers or Tchekists. I thought of a picture I had once seen in a comic paper : two burglars having broken into a house addressed the startled owners : ' You needn't be afraid, we're not from the Tcheka, we're just ordinary thieves.'

My heart was in my mouth.[1] Flight was impossible. There was nothing to do but wait. Every second seemed an eternity. The stranger downstairs went on playing. I could now recognize the melody, a well-known nocturne of Chopin. (How Radwan used to play it in Paris !) It showed the player to be an educated man ; an educated man— a Tchekist, no other explanation was possible. Never was lovely melody less welcome to the ear ; never had it hidden a more sinister message. . . . How long did it last ? A few minutes, a few hours ? Do we really require higher mathematics to prove to us the relativity of time ? One last chord—then all was quiet ; the music had stopped. It was the most critical moment of all. What would happen next ? Would they come upstairs, would they go away ?

Time passed. . . . nothing happened. . . . Silence. . . . Had they gone ?

We remained silently crouching in the darkness,

---

[1] The corresponding Russian expression uses the word ' soul ' instead of ' heart ' and ' heels ' instead of ' mouth '. Anatomically I think it is more correct. We are quite certain the heart never leaves its appointed place in the body ; as for the soul, there seems to be no reason why it should not be in the mouth, or even in the heels.

afraid to move, afraid even to breathe, listening for
the slightest sound. Silence. Then, at last, with
the utmost care, one of us crept to the door, opened
it the tiniest fraction, listened, slipped out on to the
landing. All quiet. They have gone.

I should like to say : ' We looked at each other
and burst out laughing.' It would have made an
effective epilogue. Only we didn't. Like beaten
curs we crept to our beds to seek forgetfulness in
uneasy slumber troubled by fearful dreams.

.   .   .   .   .

It is extraordinary to what an extent one's whole
appearance can be altered by a simple shawl thrown
over the head. I did not of course look like a real
peasant woman, but I could have easily been taken
for some local schoolmistress, or even the daughter
of a village priest. No other disguise was required.

Early the next morning I was on my feet. The
thought of those forty-two versts before me worked
better than any alarm-clock. Forty-two versts !

To make things worse, a decree had just been
issued forbidding the inhabitants of Petrograd to
appear in the streets after eight in the evening ;
soldiers patrolled the town demanding your documents. And if you had no documents ?

I began by resting every five versts, then every
two, then after each verst. The bag over my
shoulders grew heavier and heavier, my feet got

covered with blisters, and every muscle of my body
ached. Would I be able to do it ? From time to
time I met some troops on their way to Gatchina ;
my fears had been in vain—they never even looked
at me, never thought of stopping me or of asking me
a question. . . .

The versts grew longer and longer (the relativity
of space !) my pace grew slower and slower. Like
a pack-mule I followed the given path, without
thought or feeling, the one dull idea throbbing
through my brain—to reach Petrograd. An im-
mense lassitude filled my whole being, enveloped
me more and more with every step. . . .

Quite unexpectedly a voice sounded from behind :
' Hey, mother, where are you going ? '

Immediately I was wide awake. All trace of
fatigue had been absorbed as by a vacuum-cleaner.
My heart missed a beat ; I dared not turn round
and confront my unknown interlocutor. Was I
caught already ? Another second and I heaved a
sigh of relief. Neither the Red Army nor the Tcheka
were after me. It was a simple peasant woman,
saying good-naturedly : ' Aren't we going the same
way ? ' I felt ready to kiss the old, dirty-looking
creature. If only she were not so inquisitive. What
need had she to know both the place whence I came
and my destination ? Of what interest could the
details of my hastily-invented life be to her, a perfect
stranger ? She did not look like a secret agent, yet
it was with definite relief that I parted from her at

the next cross-roads. Poor innocent soul ! How
far we are sometimes from guessing the emotions
that some seemingly insignificant act of ours will
evoke in another's breast !

The sun was on the decline ; a cold wind swept
through the air ; the road before me was still long.
What was I to do ? It was much too cold to pass
the night out of doors ; too cold and also too
dangerous. I decided to try and get a shelter
somewhere. I knocked at the first door I came to.

' Won't you let me in for the night ? I will pay
you well.'

They hardly even listened.

' Go on, go on, *matoushka*.[1] It's a bad time for
letting strangers into the house,' and the door was
slammed in my face. It was the same at the next
house and the next. I gave it up.

There was a moment when I felt near to despair.
It seemed that no will-power could ever make me
conquer those last ten versts. Still my feet kept
on going. . . .

Several carts overtook me on the road ; each
time a momentary gleam of hope would flicker up,
only to die at once ; no pleading gesture, no
entreaty for a lift elicited the smallest sign of
sympathy on the stony faces of those drivers.

I kept on moving. The only alternative was to
lie down and die in the ditch by the roadside.
Slower and slower I advanced ; slower and slower

---

[1] *Matoushka*—little mother.

more and more painfully. At last, something like
two versts from the capital, the gods took pity on
me. A huge carriage overtook me, one of those
black and yellow *lineikas* that used to belong to the
Court Administration, and that had evidently been
confiscated by some Soviet institution. Having
just passed me, it stopped. It was not my doing—
I would never have dared to ask for help from any
Soviet officials ; simply some piece of harness had
got loose. I went up to them :

' Won't you give me a lift, comrades ? '

The faces looked far from encouraging. It was
clearly a case for stratagem. In my pocket I had
several boxes of foreign cigarettes of a good Turkish
brand ; I handed them round. Only supermen
could have resisted the temptation of a good smoke
after months of that abject stuff they call ' Soviet
makhorka '.

A few smiles appeared on the grim faces, typical
ersatz smiles. Cigarettes might be expensive in
Soviet Russia, but human sympathy could at least
be bought cheaply.

' What about that lift ? '

' Oh, well, you may come with us as far as the
city gates, but no farther.'

I had hoped for more ; the gates of the capital stood
out before me as a dangerous obstacle on my way.

Surely some kind of control had been established
there ; and I feared nothing as much as the request
to present my papers. In the company of the Soviet

5

officials I could have slipped past the guards
unnoticed.

However, better accept what was offered; so
with great alacrity I climbed on to the box, next to
the 'comrade coachman'. What a pleasure it was
to stretch my legs! At a moment's notice I could
invent no more plausible tale to satisfy the coachman's curiosity than the visit to an imaginary aunt
in Gatchina, who had suddenly been taken ill about
a fortnight ago. I had even the cheek to add some
details about my 'aunt's' illness. When the White
Army had occupied Gatchina, I had found my retreat
cut off. The story sounded quite probable.

'You have been through pretty hard times, I see,'
sympathized comrade coachman.

'You have no idea!' (There at last I was able
to put in a word of truth!)

Bravely I embarked on a fantastic recital of the
horrors of the White occupation (would the *reservatio
mentalis* I made at that moment suffice to clear me
in the eyes of the friends I was so basely calumni-
ating?) I was ready to accuse even my own family
with the worst atrocities if by so doing I could keep
up the coachman's interest in my tale. The Narva
Gates loomed before us in the dusk. A few more
lies—and we were through. A sigh of relief escaped
me. At the same moment the carriage stopped.

'Whoa, whoa,' shouted the coachman, 'time you
got down, comrade. I never noticed that we had
passed the gates.'

' Many thanks for the lift.'

How my feet hurt! How my whole body ached! I looked at my watch: already past eight. The danger of being in the streets increased every minute. I could not attempt to reach the Four-stadtskaia that night, it was much too far; and besides, I could hardly turn up at my mother-in-law's so late in the evening. A happy thought struck me. I would pass the night at the big hospital where until last spring I had worked as a doctor in one of the surgical wards. If I hurried I could be there in ten minutes. The streets were deserted, but here and there was some solitary figure on its way home. It was getting colder and colder. I hurried on, along the Zabalkansky, then down the Zagorodny. I should have to make my entry into the hospital as inconspicuous as possible; better then avoid the front entrance and try and slip in unnoticed by the back. . . . A nasty shock: the gates were already closed for the night. Only the small door under the porch was open, but I could see the watchman standing idly in the courtyard. What was I to do? Under cover of the darkness I crept up to the door and stood waiting. Several minutes passed. Would he never move? Suddenly, with a loud yawn, the man turned his back and started lazily on his rounds of the hospital buildings. The door remained open. One swift movement and I was inside. The next moment I was hurrying up the long, empty courtyard, past the women's wards, past the ward for infectious diseases, past the urological barracks. How often I had made this same round last winter when on night duty ; how well I knew every corner.

There at last was the tiny door leading to the surgical wards, next to it the window of the doctor's room. A pity the blind was down—I could not see which of the doctors was on duty. I hoped it was one of the surgeons ; the staff was so large, there were many doctors whom I hardly knew, but I would naturally only have to give my name to be recognized.

I threw a cautious look round ; all was quiet, no one seemed to have observed me. A moment to open the door, to slip through the dark corridor, then past the chief entrance, the big staircase, and the night porter, dozing peacefully in his arm-chair. Another short passage, and I was at the door of the doctor's room.

' What do you want ? Strangers are not admitted in here.' It was a lady-doctor from the medical department with whom I was but slightly acquainted. I began by declaring my identity, explained to her that I belonged to the younger surgeons. My name was, of course, familiar to her. ' But where have you come from ? At such a time and in such a state ? ' True, I had quite forgotten the shawl on my head, my dirty shoes, the bag over my shoulders.

' From London.' (I have always been unable to resist the pleasure of cheap effect.)

' What ? '

I offered her the few English biscuits left in my bag. If she had any doubts that convinced her. Not all the money in the world could have bought such biscuits in the Petrograd of those days. Later somebody told me that my lady-colleague had taken one biscuit home with her to show it to her family, and treasured it for many weeks as a reminder of a happier world.

It caused me great suffering to get the shoes off my swollen, bleeding feet. I was in a state of complete bodily exhaustion, and every single little muscle throbbed with pain. Lying down on the hard, narrow couch in the study of the head doctor, brought me a feeling of sensuous delight of such intensity as I have rarely experienced. My last conscious thought was of what awaited me on the morrow.

There are limits to physical weariness, after which no psychological worries will keep you awake. I had reached my goal, but it had not been easy. I don't believe I could do it now. I am not even sure I would try.

.   .   .   .   .

Next morning. . . . I was up with the lark. . . . In other circumstances it would have probably meant bed for three days at least, but it is a well-known fact that even a serious wound will go

unheeded in the ardour of battle. The hardest part
lay in getting on my shoes. It made me think of
Andersen's tale about the mermaid whose every
step toward her fairy prince meant agony as though
treading on sharp swords. In her days, as now,
there were neither trams nor cabs.

How strange it felt being in Petrograd once more.
I hardly noticed my surroundings ; I could think of
one thing only—what awaited me in our little
white house ?

The Fourstadtskaia. Old houses have the air
of true aristocrats ; whatever the passions raging
within them, their faces remain calm and expression-
less. Our houses had been deprived of their owners,
the furniture inside had been ruined, the walls
decorated by gross inscriptions. But outwardly
they remained the same. Nothing seemed changed
in the aspect of the white house : the windows were
unbroken, the paint was still on the walls. Only
the window-panes looked dirty, the door handle
seemed dull and unpolished, and a slight, hardly
perceptible air of neglect lay over everything. And
there, with his back to me, fiddling at the gates,
stood the old butler, who had been with the family
for over forty years.

' Good morning, Ivan Adamovitch.'

' —— ? '

' Don't you recognize me ? '

' Your Highness ! '

' How's the Prince ? '

THE 'LITTLE WHITE HOUSE' IN THE FOURSTADTSKAIA

The words were spoken. Now, in a moment, I
would know. With one word I had staked everything. Everything : the present and the future, the
happiness, the very meaning of life. What would it
be ? Heads or tails, red or black ? Somewhere the
invisible croupier had cried out : ' Rien ne va
plus.' My heart stopped beating. What would
it be : life or death ?

How long he took to answer. Was he afraid of
telling me ? ' Well ? . . .'

The old man threw a cautious look round, came
a step nearer, then in a low voice : ' Piotr Petrovitch
is in Moscow. . . .'

' Then he's alive ? . . . The whole world was
suddenly flooded with light, a loud roar filled my
ears, the houses opposite seemed to sway. . . . He's
alive !

' What's the matter ? Your Highness ! Do you
feel ill ? '

' No, no, it is over. Tell me all you know,
quickly.'

Pierre, it appeared, was in the Ivanovsky prison
camp in Moscow. He had been in prison all the
time, ever since the day of his arrest in the middle
of June. First they had taken him to the Shpalernaia prison in Petrograd, then later he had been
transferred to Moscow. News came seldom, in
the form of post cards, that he was now and then
allowed to send home. The last one had come
about a week ago ; it only said that he was in good

health, little more ; he did not complain. (As if one could complain on a post card ! As if Pierre would complain even were it possible !)

' And the old Princess, how is she ? '

My mother-in-law was in Petrograd. When the house had been seized by the Red soldiers she had been left a small building at the back of the house and had lived there ever since. For a few weeks the house had been occupied by a ballet school, then it had been taken as head-quarters for the Red Bashkir Brigade.[1] Everything in the house had been broken, spoilt, or stolen ; the books in the library used for cigarette paper, the furniture mostly burnt as fuel, the pictures cut and slashed. (Piercing the eyes of family portraits with bayonets has always been a favourite pastime of the Red warriors). The first-comers had done most of the damage ; the present occupants, the Bashkirs, behaved in a quieter way.

The old bitter feeling of resentment arose in me. So that was all Mother-in-law had achieved by refusing to go abroad : her house, all her belongings taken from her, and Pierre put into prison.

The old butler was in no hurry ; there was a great deal to tell. I interrupted him.

' Is the Princess up ? Do you think she will receive me ? '

' One moment, your Highness.'

He was soon back.

---

[1] The Bashkirs, a semi-nomad tribe in the East of Russia.

'This way, please.'

Mother-in-law was still in bed.

'Sophy!   Toi!   Est-ce possible?'

Her deafness was even more pronounced than before ; conversation was rendered extremely difficult. She showed me the latest post card from Pierre : a few sentences of perfect French, inquiring after her health, evincing anxiety for her well-being. . . . Hardly a word about himself. What a typical Pierre letter !

Mother-in-law complained of the many hardships she had to endure : the scarcity of food, the high prices of fuel. . . .

'Et que comptes-tu faire?   As-tu de l'argent?' [1]

'Pas beaucoup.   Mais il faut avant tout que je trouve où loger.' [2]

It was a broad hint ; difficult to misunderstand. The absence of identity papers put me in a very precarious position ; it would, moreover, gravely imperil the life of anyone who offered to shelter me. A very serious danger at all times, it was doubly so at the present moment, as the city was still under martial law. The Government never bluffed in questions of that kind : when it said you'd be shot, it meant just that. Did Mother-in-law know all this?   Did she understand?

'Je t'aurais naturellement offert de te loger chez moi ; mais imagine-toi quelle malchance—la lampe

[1] 'And what do you think of doing?   Have you money?'
[2] 'Not much.   But first I must find somewhere to live.'

dans la salle à manger est cassée depuis deux jours. Tu ne peux pourtant pas rester dans l'obscurité ! ' [1]

' Evidemment.' [2]

No, she had no idea of what it all meant.   A helpless old lady, cut off from all real contact with the outside world—how could she realize my desperate situation ?

' Il faut, malheureusement, que je vous quitte.' [3]

Outwardly I was calm ; it would not do to let her read in my face the hopeless thought that kept hammering through my brain : Where am I to go now ?

' Reviens me voir bien vite.' [4]

' Dès que je pourrai ' [5]

Mathilda, Mother-in-law's old maid, was waiting for me on the landing ; she had been employed in the house for nearly thirty years.

' Your Highness, your Highness, where are you going ?   Aren't you staying with us ? '

' No, Mathilda.   The Princess says it would not be convenient, because of the lamp in the dining-room.'   No need to explain, she immediately grasped the situation.

' Stay here, your Highness.   We need not tell the Princess, and we can put you up quite easily.'

' No, dear Mathilda, I cannot do that.   All the

---

[1] ' Naturally I would have offered you a room here ; but think what bad luck, for the last two days the lamp in the dining-room has been broken.   You can't possibly remain in the dark.'

[2] ' Of course.'   [3] ' I am afraid I must go now.'

[4] ' Come and see me again soon.'   [5] ' As soon as I can manage.'

same, thank you very much.   But it will be better if I find shelter elsewhere.'

' If you do not succeed, come back here.   Don't forget we can always manage it.'

Dear old soul !   What touching solicitude !   For me whom she hardly knew, who was quite a new-comer in the family.   She must have known that a person coming straight from the ' other side ', who less than a fortnight ago belonged to the White Youdenitch Army, was in the position of a hunted animal, and that if once I fell into *their* hands the proceedings would be short. . . .

First, of course, I had to find some place to live in ; then I would have to legalize my situation, procure some kind of identity papers ; after that obtain permission to go to Moscow.   It was quite clear that I could never accomplish this without outside help.   One after the other I thought of my friends : some had perished, others were abroad, others again were in prison. . . . Hardly any were left.   What about Marianna ? [1]   I had not seen her for a long time but supposed her to be in Petrograd, for I knew she had recently gone on the stage and had wholeheartedly taken up her new career.   Was she still living in the same flat, I wondered ?   What would she say on my unexpected appearance ?   I had to go to some one and could, at the moment, think of no one else.   Besides, it

[1] Countess Marianna Erikovna Zarnekau, daughter by first marriage of Princess Palei, the wife of the Grand Duke Paul.

was high time I moved on ; a man on the other side
of the street was already eyeing me suspiciously.
How long had he been there ?

.   .   .   .   .

Whenever some one says in my presence that all
human beings are nothing but dry, hard-hearted
egoists I have a ready answer : Marianna. She
owed me nothing. I was neither a relative nor a
very intimate friend. We had met at the same
parties, had dined at the same table, had more than
once passed the night together dancing or listening
to the Tziganes. She probably counted such
friends by the dozen. When I decided to go and
see her on that November morning I had no intention of asking her to shelter me ; you do not ask
people—no, not even good friends—to risk everything, including their lives, for the pleasure of
doing you a good turn. I was going to ask her for
advice, for certain useful information. Nothing
more.

Her room was on the ground floor. That made
it easier. I could knock at her window from the
street. . . .

A sleepy, bewildered face appeared behind the
curtain.

' Sophy ! You crazy being ! Where, in heaven's
name, have you dropped from ? '

A moment later I was sitting on her bed, telling
my story. Quite frankly I told her all my difficulties.

' Naturally, you are going to stay here with me. You will sleep on the couch—not very comfortable, but as there's nothing else, you'll have to rough it.'

' But, Marianna, do you understand ? I have got no identity papers, no permits. Should a search-party come to-night, you will have to share my fate. Think of it.'

' Nonsense ! We'll go and see Gorky together. I know him fairly well, and am quite sure he will not refuse you his help. He'll be able to arrange everything. As to the flat, it is all quite simple : we've got no *dvornik* [1] to the house, so for the present nobody will know you are here. Later on we will put things right with the house committee, with which I am on the best of terms.'

' Are you sure ? '

No great effort was needed to persuade me.

At a time of vast social upheavals the usual standards of life undergo a severe change ; heroism becomes an everyday occurrence, and the man who yesterday would have refused to lend his friend a sovereign will now, with hardly any hesitation, give up his life for him.

.   .   .   .   .

It was the first time I had met Gorky. A strong personality, a kind heart, a loud voice, and an

[1] Doorkeeper.

irresistible laugh—that is how he struck me. Gorky
has been greatly criticized, both as a writer and as a
politician. I am out neither to accuse nor to defend
him. (Not that he in any way needs my defence ; it
is only in the fable that the lion requires the help of
the mouse.) I know but one thing : without the
help of Gorky I should probably have perished.
Through him it was that I obtained all necessary
documents and certificates, the absence of which
placed me in danger of being arrested at every step ;
it was Gorky who arranged a few days later for my
passage to Moscow. The Revolutionary Government did not accord ordinary citizens the luxury of
travelling. Only Soviet officials—and they only
when on Government missions—had the right to a
seat in a train. At least, so it stood on paper. But
one stroke of the pen cannot overthrow the whole
structure of life nor abolish lifelong habits and
customs. All those who wished, travelled as before,
but subject to the additional inconvenience of
having to obtain an ' official mission '.

The three or four days that elapsed while waiting
for my papers to be ready were spent in frantic
activity. It is a well-known fact that virtue always
bears its own punishment, and I was now expiating
that softness of heart that had made me give so
many hasty promises to friends abroad. The
absence of any means of transport was my chief
difficulty ; the trams ran most irregularly and were
always crowded to the last inch. Cabmen had not

yet ventured out into the streets ; the few that were
to be seen demanded such high fares as the reward
of their courage that only the most sincere Communists could afford them.   Besides, cabmen being an
institution invented by the *bourgeoisie,* were considered undesirable in a Communist State.   The
species soon died out, only to flourish anew two
years later when the clever move called the introduction of the N E P ruined Communism but
saved the Communists ;   theory was sacrificed that
individual power might be retained.

In the meantime nothing remained to the inhabitants of the capital but to go on foot.   Even short
distances seem to spread out indefinitely when
measured by one's own footsteps.   I sincerely pity
the citizens of London if some future Communist
revolution in England does away with all means
of transport.   London is so much larger than
Petrograd.

I would have shown greater intelligence had I
looked after my own affairs instead of giving up so
much time to visiting places and people whom I
often did not even know.   One or two broken
promises would not have made any great difference
to me on the day of the Last Judgment.

But how could I, for instance, forgo to visit the
mother of a well-known ' White ' general, who for
many months had been unable to send her even
a single word of greeting ?   How omit to take her
his message, to let her know that he was abroad,

alive and well, his only worry being for her safety ?
I remember so well the look of distrust, even of
fear, with which the poor old lady opened the door
and listened to my tale.   A perfect stranger saying
she had come from *him*, had seen him, had even
talked to him not so very long ago . . . and the
fleeting thought so clearly mirrored in her eyes :
' How do I know ? she may be an *agent provocateur*
from the Tcheka.' . . . And then, later, when she
had at last been convinced and no longer distrusted
me, the change that came over her whole being,
the radiance that illuminated her face at the joyful
tidings I had brought her, the words of gratitude,
the questions with which she overwhelmed me,
while she furtively wiped away the tears that kept
falling softly from her eyes.

At another place in answer to my knock (the
door-bells had for the most part ceased to work),
the door was opened not by the young lady I was
seeking but by a fierce-looking sailor.

' What do you want ? '

' Tell me, please, who is living here now ? '

Of course I mentioned no names. *Nomina odiosa
sunt*. Here, names were dangerous. It was a
favourite trick of the Tcheka, when it put some one
into prison, to make a kind of trap out of the arrested
person's rooms ; all those who called were sent to
join their friend in prison.   No exception was made
for the doctor calling on his sick patient, nor a
neighbour coming to borrow a handful of salt—all

explanations would in due course be given to the
prison authorities. Sometimes this little game went
on for weeks. One had to be very cautious when
inquiring for an absent friend. This time my
doubts were soon at an end.

' Have you no eyes,' shouted the sailor angrily.
' Didn't you see the board outside stating that this
is a sailors' club in the name of comrade Lenin ?
If every idiot imagines she may disturb people for
nothing . . .'

But I listened no more. A hasty few strides had
taken me down the stairs and into the street as the
angry bang of the door resounded loudly through
the house. I have never learnt what happened to
the lady I wanted to see. Had she left town, was
she dead, or in prison ? To this day I have not
the slightest idea.

.   .   .   .   .

From the first I had been longing to go to my
old flat on the English Quay ; but caution restrained
me. All the houses in Petrograd had been confiscated by the State ; the doorkeepers, receiving
no more pay, had left, and the front entrances in
most houses had been closed. In those days all
Petrograd used the back staircase. The back entrance to my flat was through the Galernaia Street,
at the same end of which were the houses of my
father, and also of my first husband's family. Every
cat down there knew me by sight. If I showed

6

myself there now, some one would be sure to recognize me, and that had better be avoided until my papers were in order and I was ready to face the authorities.   When in the autumn of 1918 I married Pierre and went to live with him at the Fourstadtskaia, Eses took over my flat.   Later, Eses went abroad and only my maid Natasha and her husband remained to look after the flat.   They were protected by a paper which Eses, in his quality of foreign diplomat, had been able to nail on the door. The value of that paper lay in the fact that the integrity of the flat was guaranteed by the signature of Lenin himself.

That was six months ago.   What had taken place since then ?   Was my true friend Natasha still there ?   A few guarded inquiries brought me the information I wanted :   the flat had not been touched ;   Natasha had committed suicide.

What ?   Natasha had committed suicide ?   Forgetting all precautions I hurried to the owner of our house, the wife of General Chekessoff, who lived in the flat beneath mine.   From her I would be able to learn all the details.

Yes, it was true.   Natasha had hung herself one night, soon after I had left.   On the fatal evening she had quarrelled with her husband, had then shut herself up in her room and was not seen again alive. The nail in the wall was so low that to achieve her purpose she had been obliged to double up her legs. . . .

THE HOUSE IN ST. PETERSBURG WHERE I WAS BORN
(GARDEN SIDE)

OWNED BY MY LATE FATHER, COUNT BOBRINSKOY, FORMER IMPERIAL
MINISTER OF AGRICULTURE

'And what about Michael, her husband? He was so deeply devoted to her!'

'He was in a terrible state. It was he who found her; her body was still warm. When he opened the door he saw her standing quietly in the dark corner. He spoke to her but got no answer. Then he saw. His screams woke the whole house. We all came running to the spot, while he kept on screaming and screaming. It was simply frightful. The doctor feared for his reason. He could not go on living in those rooms, haunted by that terrible memory, so he left town and went back to his village. The other day somebody coming from there brought the news of his engagement to one of the local beauties. But that may not be true—you know how people will gossip.'

So that was it. Poor Natasha, with her big black eyes and an air of general refinement, so unusual in a person in her station. I could not get rid of a certain feeling of guilt. She had come to me last spring, just before my departure, complaining of a general feeling of depression and misery. Why had I taken her words so lightly? How could I have so completely misjudged the gravity of her case? I, a doctor! How dense are our perceptions! I talked with a nervously overwrought house-maid, and never suspected that the woman before me was on the brink of despair. She complained of depression, true, but who was not depressed in those days? Are there not many among us who have been miserable ever since ? Perhaps she has chosen the happier lot.

How I enjoyed being once more in my old flat. All so quiet, so beautiful, all my things in their own places. I opened the drawers, sorted some papers, looked through old letters. Love letters, of course. No others are worth keeping ; are hardly ever worth writing. Why is it most love letters are so silly ? The stronger the emotions, the duller seems to grow the intellect. Whereas sweet sentimental outpourings can be found by the dozen, there is nothing so rare as a witty expression of sexual desire. By some occult law, sentiment seems to act as inhibitor to the activity of the brain. In all my life I came across only two or three exceptions to the rule.

I ought to have remained in Petrograd a little longer to take care of my flat, and found some reliable person to live there and look after my things. Later I was bitterly to regret my carelessness in omitting to do so. I could have saved everything. But I decided to trust the signature of Lenin on the paper protecting my flat. The idea of trusting Lenin's promise ! It served me right.

True, no material advantages, no treasure in the world could have tempted me then to put off my departure to Moscow, even for a few hours. In Moscow I would see Pierre. . . .

On reaching Petrograd I sent Pierre a post card ;

prisoners were allowed a certain limited correspondence with their friends and relatives outside.
I wrote only a few words, so that he should know
I was near and was coming to the rescue. For
some unknown reason the prison authorities were
suspicious, and my post card never reached him.
Thus, when we met, my presence was totally
unexpected. Fate was keeping up the element of
surprise to enhance the effect of our meeting. Life
can sometimes play the part of stage-manager as
cleverly as Mr. Lioubich.

'The wolf will always come back to the wood,
no matter how well you feed him,' were the
words with which Vladimir Casimirovitch greeted
me.

Vladimir Casimirovitch, he whom Diogenes had
all his life looked for in vain.

I had counted on bringing Pierre my London box
with dry provisions which I had left in Gatchina in
charge of Mrs. Pousseff. The chief difficulty lay
in getting the box from Gatchina to Petrograd.
One day Marianna said : 'An officer whom I know
is going to Gatchina to-morrow by car. If you
wish he'll bring back your box.' Splendid ! At
once I wrote a note to Mrs. Pousseff asking her to
deliver the box to Mr. So-and-So. Alas ! some
temptations are *Über unsere Kraft*. Never again did
I see either my box or Marianna's officer-friend.

Who are they who unknown to me enjoyed my
treasure ? Will the memory of that deed torment
them on their death-bed ? I hope so with all my
heart. All my efforts, all my sacrifices, all the
difficulties I had overcome in my endeavours to
keep the box safe and intact—all had been in vain.
' Tout comprendre c'est tout pardonner,' said Mme.
de Stael. I had no difficulty in understanding. As
to forgiving—no, I cannot even now forgive the
man whose greed deprived Pierre of those few
delicacies—the only comfort I could offer him after
five months of semi-starvation in a Soviet prison.

.   .   .   .   .

Meanwhile, with the help of Gorky, I had obtained
permission to travel to Moscow. The certificate
stated that I was being sent to Moscow on an
official mission in the quality of a music instructress ;
a number of signatures and seals gave the paper an
imposing aspect, and procured me the right of
travelling first class, with that minimum of comfort
which was denied to ordinary mortals. The word
' comfort ' must not bring to mind a warm Pullman
car, with a couch to lie on, clean bed-linen, etc.
All the ' comfort ' I could expect would be a seat
in an unheated compartment, the air thick with the
breath of the seven other passengers tightly packed
together. But at least I had a seat, and the
possibility of getting up, going into the corridor,

visiting the lavatory or procuring a glass of hot
water at the station. What went on in the other
carriages, where passengers were denied even
this, I shall not attempt to describe ; moreover, it
has been described often enough.

The secret irony of my situation lay in my complete lack of any musical training. The wrecked
nerves of half a dozen music-mistresses had been
unable to endow me with an ear for rhythm.
Luckily, nobody asked me to display my musical
talents, and the document led me safely past all
control officers and barriers. May God grant
Gorky a happy and serene old age ! Next day I
was in Moscow.

.   .   .   .   .

I was now in quite a different situation from that in
which I had been when I first reached Petrograd.
All my papers, certificates, permits were in order ;
once more I felt like a human being. It is no
exaggeration to say that in those days the absence
of necessary documents made you an outcast. Not
only were you in constant danger of arrest and
prison, but every step was surrounded with difficulties ; you would be equally unable to find either
a meal or a roof, for no one (unless a devoted and
fearless friend like Marianna) would let you in for
the night ; and after eight o'clock you would be
arrested for being in the streets. Now, at least, I

could without trembling pass the ' militia-man ' [1] posted at the corner of the street.   It is on purpose that I use the word ' militia ' ; a Tchekist would always remain an object of fear, to me as to everybody else.

At Moscow I went straight from the station to the Cheremetevski Pereoulok ; I had been told Prince Serge Wolkonsky was living there.   Serge was a first cousin of Pierre's, a writer of a certain renown, a fervent admirer of Dalcrosa's system of rhythmical gymnastics, and formerly the Director of the Imperial Theatres.   I knew him but slightly ; I do not think we had met more than three or four times in all.   I knew that my arrival could hardly be welcome.   The small flat already held five people ; I was the sixth.   None of the others had ever even seen me ; unasked, unexpected, I dropped into their midst.   One cold November afternoon I rang at their door.

' I am the wife of Pierre and have just arrived in Moscow to try and rescue him from prison.   I've nowhere to live.   Will you take me in ? '

' Naturally.'

They gave me one of their rooms ; it was neither agreeable nor convenient for them, but they did it without a moment's hesitation.   I hated being a nuisance but I had no choice ; there was nothing

---

[1] The revolution had abolished the police ; a great number had been killed, others had fled ; the militia formed in its place was naturally much inferior.

else to do. Hotels did not exist, there were no
apartments or rooms to let ; all restaurants had
been closed, all shops abolished. You were not
allowed to buy either a piece of bread or a pair of
stockings—not even a button. . . . Mad days, life
upside down. The realm of topsy-turvydom. A
nightmare fantasy of Wells come true. Even now
we sometimes ask ourselves : Can it really have
been ?

.   .   .   .   .

From Lisette I learnt that visitors were admitted
to the Ivanosky prison camp only once a week—on
Sundays. On Wednesday one could transmit to the
prisoners parcels of food, but only through the
guard. Personal meetings were restricted to once
a week.

Long before the appointed time I had taken my
place in the long queue at the prison gates. It was
composed of a pitiful crowd, mostly the former
possessors of a good place in the show of life, whom
the revolution had reduced to a state of abject
poverty. Yellow skins, hungry eyes, faces marked
by the blows of fate, stamped by terror of Dzerjinsky[1]

At the moment, however, I had no thought for
them. One casual glance at the sea of human
misery round me, then I forgot them. Somewhere

[1] Felix Dzerjinsky, the all-powerful chief of the Tcheka, and probably
the most detested man in all Russia. He died of heart failure some years
ago.

a clock had struck the quarter. The reception began at two. It is difficult to wait patiently when all your thoughts and feelings are in a turmoil; when you feel at the same time like dancing for joy and crying for misery. . . . Feverishly I counted the minutes. Then, suddenly my heart dashed into a furious two-step. The gates were being slowly opened.

The meetings took place in a small courtyard, under the supervision of an armed guard. The prisoners were led out in groups of about twenty, to meet a corresponding number of visitors. In a few seconds the yard was overcrowded. The air resounded with a loud murmur of voices; there was a great deal of jolting and pushing each other out of the way as each one hurried to find his friends among the crowd.

At the first glance I hardly recognized him: the thin face, the long hair, the small beard he had let grow—it felt like looking at a stranger. . . . He had not yet caught sight of me. His eyes were searching the crowd, expecting to see either Lisette or Elena Nikolaievna; the idea that it could be me naturally never entered his head. Did he not know me to be miles away, somewhere in England? 'Hullo!' He turned round, a perplexed expression on his face. Our eyes met. A momentary doubt, then he understood; stretched out his arms: 'But it is absurd!'

What can one say to each other, after six months

of separation, during a mere quarter of an hour, standing on the snow among a noisy crowd, surrounded by eavesdropping strangers, followed incessantly by the suspicious gaze of the prison guards. . . . What can one say ? Detached words, broken sentences, a few short questions. We understood each other without speaking. One look, one touch of the hand, and all was said. The sound of a harsh voice broke the spell.

' Time is up, citizens. Visitors are requested to leave at once.' Hurried embraces, confusion ; couples torn asunder, pushed roughly towards the door. All the things I ought to have discussed with Pierre, all the important matters we were to have talked over, come rushing to my mind. All the many questions I wanted to ask him. ' Hurry up, you there ! Haven't you heard the command ? ' One had to obey.

' Good-bye, God bless you, darling.'

' Till next Sunday.'

Joy—misery ; sadness—happiness. . . . Our language is made up of simple formulae and ignores the subtle complexities of human emotions. I was both happy and miserable : happy that I had overcome all difficulties, had reached him, had talked to him, and would now be able to ease, if only a little, the hardships of his lot. I could hardly believe I was really in Moscow. The strange, fantastic city, unlike any other town in the world. I knew it but slightly, yet every Russian feels at home in Moscow.   It made me happy to be back in my country, to see Russian faces, hear Russian speech.   Then I thought of Pierre : of his wan face, the unhealthy pallor of his skin—the effects of hunger and physical privations.   I clenched my fists in impotent rage, as I thought of the five months he had been made to suffer in the dirt and squalor of an overcrowded cell, forced to sleep night after night without undressing, lying on the floor or on the hard planks of a wooden seat.   And added to this the hunger, the cold, the lack of washing accommodation, the absence of decent lavatories, the stinking pail that infested the air of the cell during the night. . . . The world has been told over and over again of the horrors of Soviet prisons ; but it is one thing to read about it, sitting comfortably in an arm-chair near the fire, and another to know that the person nearest to you in the world is himself, hour after hour, undergoing all the sufferings of slow torture. . . . The moral suffering was perhaps the hardest to bear : the rudeness of the guards, the everyday petty humiliations, the mocking glances and cutting words of those who were glad to see their former masters humbled in the dust.   And, above all, the constant menace of a summary execution, the sudden brutal death that had taken away so many of his friends and prison comrades.   To think that it was Pierre on whom all this suffering was inflicted : gentle, refined Pierre, whose whole being shrank from a rough gesture or a rude word! How I hated them! A puny, harmless hate, humiliating in its impotence, its useless, innocuous craving for revenge!

I feared the future; was tormented by the thought of all the difficulties, the uncertainty, the danger that lay in store for us. There was no Madame de Thèbes [1] I could consult. The struggle I would have to undertake against the Tcheka in order to get Pierre released would be no easy one. The forces were uneven. What would be the issue of the contest in which Pierre's head was to play the part of conventional silver goblet as prize to the winner?

.   .   .   .

My unexpected appearance in the prisoners' camp had not passed unnoticed; the whole prison was impressed. It hardly ever happened that some one of his own accord returned to Soviet Russia. But that a wife should come back from abroad in order to rescue her husband—such a fact had never yet occurred.

A curious incident happened to me a day or two later. I had decided to apply to Commissar Medvedev, chief administrator of all Moscow prisons and ask him for an extra interview with my husband. Whilst waiting in Medvedev's anteroom I entered into conversation with my neighbour, a simple-looking peasant woman. It so happened that the

[1] Madame de Thèbes, the famous Parisian clairvoyant.

woman had only that same morning been released from the Ivanovsky [1] prison camp. Why it was called 'camp' I never discovered. A former monastery turned hastily into a prison, it had nothing at all of a camp about it.

I was naturally much interested, for there were quite a number of details I was eager to learn concerning prison life—the amount and quality of the food, the way prisoners were treated, etc. The woman proved talkative.

'Just imagine,' said she, 'what happened the other day : they've got a prince, there at the camp, and—would you believe it ?—his wife came back to him from abroad ! What do you say to that ! '

'Impossible ! '

She got quite angry with me for my alleged doubts. ' Some of our people even saw her ! ' . . .

There is a kind of peculiar pleasure in listening anonymously to a story about oneself, especially if one is made to play the part of heroine. It has all the charm of eavesdropping, unpoisoned by the fear of detection. I was preparing to draw her on, and to enjoy the situation to the full, when the door opened and I was called away. The commissar being absent it was his lady secretary who received the applicants. I never thought one human heart could harbour so much malice.

' Why do you ask for an extra interview ? '

' I have not seen my husband for half a year.'

[1] Ivanovsky : the official name was ' Ivan Camp of Forced Labour '.

' So—so, a former prince. . . . A bit of prison life will do him, and such as he, no end of good.'

' ? '——

' In old times you certainly never thought of those you were bleeding to death behind prison bars. You persecuted and oppressed the people whilst you yourself wallowed in luxury and idleness.'

' I assure you I never persecuted anybody.'

' Now you will learn for yourself how it feels having to bow your head and beg for mercy. You need not expect any indulgence from me ! '

A veritable she-devil ! A Communist ogress ! Well, at least I knew where I stood. She would never grant my request—I might as well return the way I came. As luck would have it, at the same moment the commissar made his appearance. Of quiet demeanour, with a pale, ascetic face and a clever look in his big black eyes, he presented a complete contrast to his secretary. On hearing my plea he at once ordered the necessary permit to be issued. Later on I had to apply to him several times and always met with the same quiet courtesy, the same absence of all useless words. If only all Bolsheviks were like him ! The revelation of his true character came to me much later : the soft voice, the charming manners were but a mask covering the ruthlessness of Torquemada, a ferocity equalling that of Ghenghis Khan. The sobs of a mother, the prayers of a wife had never been able to touch him, never once had his hand trembled when signing a death-warrant. Even those in the Tcheka feared him. . . . No, better a hundred jeering secretaries than this one man with the face of an ascetic and the soul of an executioner.

.   .   .   .   .

There is a book called *From a Russian Diary 1917–1920* by an Englishwoman.[1] On page 243 the author, whom I have never met in my life, records the fact of my arrival in Moscow from abroad, of which she had heard from a friend. The book now occupies an important place on my book-shelf. . . . Silly vanity ? I have many other faults as well as vanity . . . thus, I always stop to observe dogs fighting in the street, I cross on to the other side when from afar I catch sight of a beggar ; I never see an aeroplane without secretly hoping that I may witness its fall. . . . The list could be easily prolonged. However, writing memoirs does not mean making a confession. Far from it. Luckily.

Now that I was in Moscow, I at once began to work out a plan for getting Pierre out of prison. I had no illusions ; I knew it would be difficult, but I also knew that I would not give up trying until I had achieved my purpose. My plan was roughly as follows :

All through the previous winter Pierre had worked

[1] London, John Murray, 1921.

for the ' Vsemirnaia Literatoura ' (' The Literature
of the World '), a Soviet institution under the
patronage of Gorky, the unofficial aim of which was
to save from hungry death all that remained of the
literary circles of Petrograd. It came as near to
open charity as the situation allowed. Surely much
will be forgiven Gorky because of his initiative in
that matter. Under the thin pretext of translating
all the literary masterpieces of the whole world, a
small allowance was doled out to those Russian
writers who would have otherwise been on the brink
of starvation. Excepting one or two who had
gone over to the side of the victors, the whole
Russian intelligentsia had been deprived of its means
of existence. Pierre had also applied for work and
had been given Endymion to translate. ' A thing
of beauty is a joy for ever.' . . . What would Keats
have said had he seen what an instrument of torture
had been made out of his beautiful poem ? Night
after night Pierre toiled conscientiously, breaking
his head in search of a missing rhyme. It requires
real poetical talent to make even a passable transla-
tion of a foreign poet, the more so when you are
asked to do it in rhymed verse. And Keats is
especially difficult—so at least he seemed to us
then. For Pierre the point lay not so much in the
ridiculously small pay he got as in the document
which admitted him to the class of ' intellectual
workers ' ; one simply could not exist without some
certificate of the kind. But the zeal he put into his

7

work was quite superfluous ; nobody paid the least
attention to the quality of his verse ; probably
nobody ever read it. It would be interesting to
know what happened to all those hundreds upon
hundreds of written sheets, composed with so much
labour by a lot of half-starved, miserable beings.
They are probably still lying on the same spot
where they were thrown twelve years ago—vast piles
of waste-paper in some garret on the Mokhovaia.

But to return to my plan. I had obtained from
Gorky a kind of certificate showing that Pierre had
worked under him in the ' Vsemirnaia Literatoura ',
and was in consequence a useful member of society.
At my request Gorky also signed a paper stating
that he knew Pierre personally and was ready to
vouch for his inoffensiveness in regard to the Soviet
Republic. This paper would undoubtedly help me
in my dealings with the authorities. But it would
not help much. Gorky was known to have shielded
so many, his name had been so often used as a
lever in opening the prison doors, that his signature
had lost a great deal of its original value. A psychological *chèque sans provision.* Now, the signature
of a man like Krassin would produce a far greater
effect ; but it was also ever so much more difficult
to obtain. Would I be able to get it ? . . . I had
certain reasons for believing that Krassin would not
refuse my request ; for although I had been obliged
to destroy the precious letter Eses had given me
for him (please do not imagine, dear V., that I have

forgotten all you made me suffer !), I knew that in my coming talk with Krassin the name of Eses would be a very definite trump-card in my hands. I felt sure that if handled with a certain skill, and with just a reasonable amount of luck, the situation ought to give the required result. And so it proved.

The first difficulty was to obtain an interview with Krassin. No Tsar, no Eastern potentate ever surrounded himself with as many barriers as a leader of the triumphant proletariat.[1]

It was as difficult to obtain a glimpse of Lenin's face (in the pre-mausoleum period of his biography) as it would have been to gaze on the unveiled charms of Abdul Hamid's favourite wife.

I visited all the places where I might have even the slightest chance of meeting Krassin—his room at the Soviet hotel, the various institutions which counted him among its members, the bureaux he worked in. I would sometimes have to traverse the whole town on foot (it was not only a question of economy : no other means of transport existed),

---

[1] I have it on the authority of such a man as Savinkoff, through the intermediary of a mutual friend ; and Savinkoff, who had made political assassinations his profession, ought to know. According to him, the rarity of political murders nowadays in Russia, as compared to the great number under the former regime, is due to the physical impossibility for any outsider gaining access to the Bolshevik leaders. Combining methods of the Tsarist police with the ruses and experience of lifelong revolutionaries, the Bolsheviks have succeeded in entrenching themselves behind a nearly perfect conspiracy-proof system. Savinkoff lost his life in looking for some leak in the system. Perhaps others will prove luckier.

would then wait for several hours in a stuffy ante-room full of unwashed, underfed people, only to hear the announcement that ' In view of the late hour, Comrade Krassin will not receive anyone '. Dejectedly I would tramp all the way back, firmly resolved to return next week.

At last I succeeded in finding him one early morning at the Hôtel Metropole. Formerly one of the smartest hotels in Moscow, it had now been transformed into rooms for the great ones in the Communist world : ' The Second Soviet House.' But old names are tenacious : ' the Hôtel Metro-pole ' remained the ' Hôtel Metropole '. No decree could force the population to adopt the new language. It was the same thing with the newly-renamed streets ; the same with our titles, officially abolished, but by which even the Bolsheviks themselves kept addressing us.   What's in a name ?   More than we think, perhaps.   An empty sound has often proved more resisting, more difficult to destroy than a great structure of iron and stone.

' Yes, Commissar Krassin is in his room.'   But it was not as simple as that.   Nobody was allowed into the building without a written permit, which one had to give up on leaving, and without which you would not be allowed out of the house.   I wrote down my name, the person I wanted to see, the reason of my visit. . . . The telephone rang. ' The Commissar will see you.'   I was allowed to pass.

His manner was perfectly courteous.   I told him

I had just returned from abroad, where I had seen Eses, and that I was now acting according to the latter's instructions—in case of any serious difficulty to apply to him, Krassin. I mentioned the letter Eses had given me, but which caution had obliged me to destroy. I further told him of how Pierre had been arrested nearly six months ago and was condemned to stay in prison as hostage until the end of the civil war. My one hope was in him. . . . He was very amiable, full of sympathy, promised to make the necessary inquiries, and to see what could be done. . . . It was, of course, most kind of him. But I knew too well these vague promises of future help. I needed something more definite. I thanked him profusely, said how grateful I would be for any help, but there was also something else : and pulling out the paper by which Gorky guaranteed Pierre's innocence of any plotting against the Soviets, I asked him to add his signature. ' Leave it with me. I will think it over.' He could have flatly refused ; his not having done so was in itself something of a victory. I left him full of hope.

We lived through the winter of 1920 in Moscow. Only those who have experienced it will understand. As to the others—no description will ever give them an adequate idea.

Yes, of course, we suffered from hunger. In a lesser degree than many others : we had a meal every day, sometimes even twice a day. And

yet. . . . Without meat, without butter, or sugar,
or white flour or fresh vegetables. . . . Frozen
potatoes and millet cooked in water (the kind of
grain Europeans give their poultry). Nothing else,
day after day. Whatever one did, the thought of
food never left one ; was constantly there, somewhere at the back of one's mind. It became an
obsession, and, like all fixed ideas, upset one's whole
mental balance.

From time to time, after dark, strange people
with bags behind their backs knocked stealthily at
the kitchen door : the one offered flour, the other
had a sack of potatoes, or perhaps even a bit of
butter. They bargained in whispers, threw cautious
glances all round them before leaving the house. . . .
True, nearly anything could be bought from the
street vendors stationed round the former market-
places, if only one did not mind the risk of being
caught in a police raid, and either fined heavily, or,
more often, put in prison for ' illicit speculation '.
Bread traffic was for some reason a special feature
of the Moscow University ; it was carried on by
the numerous attendants in the underground pas-
sages of the huge building. You had to wait till
evening, then slip quietly along the deserted streets,
knock at the stipulated door. . . . A little later you
would hurry home by the shortest way, the newly-
bought loaf hidden under your coat, and the smell
of the heavy, damp, black bread irresistibly teasing
your tormented senses. Every shadow made you

start : you were committing an illegal act punishable by law.

Food was our constant preoccupation ; the one all-absorbing topic of every conversation : where, for how much, of what quality. . . . An operation was being performed in one of the town hospitals ; the peritoneum had been cut open, the bowels laid out. Some one in the room mentioned the price of butter. The surgeon took it up, the assistant-surgeon replied. The operation went on ; the hands of the surgeon ran automatically along the bowels, the assistant mechanically caught the squirting blood-vessels, the nurse presented the instruments—while the all-important discussion on butter went on uninterrupted. I have not invented the story. I myself was present. I was the assistant.

We also suffered from cold. Here again we were better off than many others : the temperature in our rooms never dropped below four or five degrees (Réaumur) ;[1] in the morning we did not have to break the ice in the jug before taking a wash ; not even during the severest frosts.

We never took off our fur coats ; we sat in them by day and slept in them by night. Reading was difficult ; the hands that held the book kept freezing, whilst with gloves on you could not turn the pages. Sewing was even harder, for the fingers were numb with cold and refused to manipulate the needle. There was nothing left but to forgather miserably

[1] 4° Réaumur = 37° Fahrenheit.

round the small kitchen stove and evoke for the hundredth time the memories of happier days. But it often happened that even the kitchen stove was cold.

The only housemaid had left several weeks ago. No one but Communists could afford the luxury of a servant : we had to do all the work ourselves. Hard work. We took turns in cooking the dinner, in heating the stove, in washing up. One of the hardest tasks consisted in bringing the big, heavy logs of wood up the stairs, all the way from the garage, and sawing them into small pieces. When during the fourth year of my medical training we learnt to perform amputations on corpses, the Professor used to say : ' The technique is quite simple ; saw the bone in the same way as you saw a log of wood.' Possibly, the other girls knew how to saw wood. For myself the experience was reversed ; when my saw got stuck in one of those big frozen logs, I tried to think of the operating table : the same movement as when sawing through the tibia.

Worse was to come. As a result of the great frost, all water-pipes burst in the insufficiently heated houses. For many weeks we were obliged to fetch the water from the next-door courtyard. It was no joking matter ; there was always a long queue standing before the pump—at all hours of the day, but especially long close to lunch- and dinner-time ; quite like the Paris underground *aux heures d'affluence*. One's hands and toes grew

stiff with cold. . . . At last you found yourself at
the pump, your pail overflowing with icy water,
your last pair of boots getting soaked through and
through while you stood in the large pool that
spread all round the pump.   Then came the return
journey with the heavy pail full of water, up the
narrow, dark staircase covered with a slippery coat
of ice, the inevitable result of overflowing water.
The same thing had to be repeated twice, sometimes
three times a day.   But what right had we to
complain ?   We lived on the second floor . . . what
about those who lived on the fifth ?

We had no men to help us with the heavy work.
We were five women in that flat, with Serge the
only man.   But Serge was out lecturing nearly all
day, and usually returned late in the evening ; so
we saw but little of him.   The four other inmates
consisted of Elena Nikolaievna, her sixteen-year-
old daughter Olga, Lisette—Serge's beautiful young
niece (also second cousin of my husband) and old
Nadejda Amandovna, left to look after the flat by
its former owners, who as far as I know, had
emigrated abroad.

Sometimes we quarrelled.   The reasons were
mostly insignificant ; more often there would be no
reason at all.   If one thinks of the life we led, the
privations we endured, the small space we had to
live in, and the importance of each one doing her
full share of the work, it is a wonder we did not
quarrel a great deal more.

The evenings were very dull. As a rule the
electric current was cut off in the whole town long
before bed-time; it is impossible to sit alone in a
dark, bitterly cold room with nothing but your own
gloomy thoughts to keep you company. We usually
sat in the kitchen, round the dying embers in
the tiny cooking-stove. Some friend living in the
neighbourhood would perhaps drop in for a talk.
Our conversation varied but little: news of the
latest arrests, rumours of So-and-So having been
shot; endless talk about food, discussions about
the way of procuring provisions, the ever-augmenting
prices; the comparative value of the different
rations served out to their staffs by various Soviet
institutions. The pastime I most hated was the
composing of imaginary menus: the elaborate
dinners one hoped to eat some day—a kind of self-
torture or mental flagellation most of us indulged
in periodically. All other topics had been either
exhausted or had long ago lost interest. Each knew
by heart what the other was going to say. Thus in
war-time, during the long periods of inactivity at
the front, we used to get to know all the gramophone
records of our Red Cross unit: always the same
tunes, by day and by night, over and over again,
till some of us grew furious and others got desperate,
and the news of an impending battle came as a
long-awaited distraction.

It became every day more and more difficult to

keep oneself clean. The grey horror—lice—found their way into every house. Time and again did I happen to discover one in my clothes ; the first time I was sick with disgust and nearly burst out crying. For long I struggled, revolted against the inevitable ; tried all the measures I had heard of. I rubbed my whole body with a stuff the smell of which would have turned the stomach of a whale ; for many weeks I wore a small bag containing some unknown charm on a string round my neck ; camphor oil, naphthaline—there was nothing I left untried. I even went the length of washing every morning, however great the cold, and of changing my underwear as often as my means permitted. . . . It was all of no avail. Both science and superstition proved powerless against the foe. So I gave up the useless struggle and accepted my fate with the meekness of a Ghandi. One can get accustomed even to vermin on one's body. True, I cannot boast of having ever reached the same degree of philosophical resignation as those who passed the time by betting whether the quantity of insects gathered with one sweep of the hand would prove an even or uneven number. They say the game was a very popular one—especially amongst prisoners . . . The harder grew the general conditions of life, the greater became the scourge of dirt, lice, and epidemics. Even Lenin got alarmed. For a few weeks the streets were covered with enormous picture placards : ' Is the louse going to conquer

Communism ? ' And the passers-by sent up a silent prayer to Heaven that the monsters would destroy each other.

Alongside of our common duties in the flat, each one of us had her own private worries. For my part, all my thoughts and all my efforts concentrated round one thing only : Pierre. My first duty was to keep him from dying of hunger ; being reduced to prison rations meant a slow but sure death from exhaustion.

On Sundays I brought him food personally. On Wednesdays it could only be transmitted through the guard ; the parcel could be accompanied by a short list of the things it contained ; either through the negligence of the guards or because of their illiteracy, a few words of correspondence could safely be added to the list. We were never caught, although officially all correspondence uncontrolled by the authorities was prohibited. Pierre did the same when returning me the empty dishes. I have kept several of these notes, written on scraps of coarse grey paper. Here are a few of them, translated word for word ; they seem to give a vivid illustration of the times I am trying to describe.

The first, chronologically, is a post card dated November 20th 1919, a few days after my arrival at Moscow :

Wednesday, after the meeting :

Do not overwhelm me by ruining yourself to get food for me. There is too much of *everything*. God grant we will meet again on Sunday. Only, please, don't bring me anything ; or just two or three pieces of black bread and perhaps something to smoke. Greetings to the Cheremetevsky Pereoulok, and thanks to every one. Already on Sunday comparisons were drawn here with the ' Russian Women ' by Nekrassoff.[1]

With the prayer to take care of yourself and with hope.

SECRETARY TO THE LIBRARY.[2]

From P. P. Wolkonsky, Wednesday, December 10th, 1919.
Corridor VII, Cell 80.

One net bag,
One bottle,
Thank you.
Am nourishing the body and also hope.
Be well and careful.
Good-bye.

From P. P. Wolkonsky, Wednesday, January 14th, 1920.
Corridor VII, Cell 80.   *Return Parcel.*

1 net bag.
1 bottle,
1 pair of drawers with the prayer to return them later on.

Forgive me last Sunday's behaviour. I was not well and spent yesterday, Tuesday, in bed. All right again to-day.

---

[1] ' Russian Women,' a classical poem by Nekrassoff which tells the story of Princess Wolkonsky, wife of the *dekabrist* or partaker in the conspiracy of December 1825, who followed her husband to Siberia.

[2] By doctor's order Pierre had been freed from manual labour and appointed instead secretary to the prison library.

Got awfully sad post card from Mother. (' Loneliness and
pain have broken my spirit.') I wonder whether one
could not put her in some hospital. But I'm afraid she
would not consent.[1] We have now passed definitely into
the year 1920.[2] I can ask no greater *happiness* for myself
than that already given me—but only for the *joy* of being
near you. But it hurts me to think of you and Mother. I
wish you happiness. Hope to see you on Sunday.

From P. P. Wolkonsky, January 21st, 1920.

Corridor VII, Cell 80.   *Return Parcel.*

1 net bag,
1 round pot,
1 bottle,
The toast was excellent. . . .
Would you like the idea of trying to send message to your
daughter by applying to the English parson, Reverend North,
Big Tchernyshevsky Pereoulok 8 ? (Not far from you.)
I saw letters arrived *from there* [3] that took hardly a month.
(Litvinoff's channel.)
However
(1) I don't know when the next departure *from here* will
take place.
(2) There may be *awful* danger (ambuscade, etc.) ; so *if*
you do it, better try through Valia (or after Cony's [4] return.)
No news from anywhere. Thinking constantly and
feeling deeply with the poor freezing Bird. Thanks.

[1] In English in the original.
[2] The ' old style ' Russian New Year is thirteen days later than in
Western Europe.
[3] ' From there ' means from England. A month is considered an
extraordinarily short time for a letter from England to reach Moscow.
[4] Count Constantine Benckendorff, son of the late Russian Ambassador
in London.

PIERRE, FIRST ON THE LEFT, WORKING IN THE PRISON LIBRARY,
WINTER, 1919–20

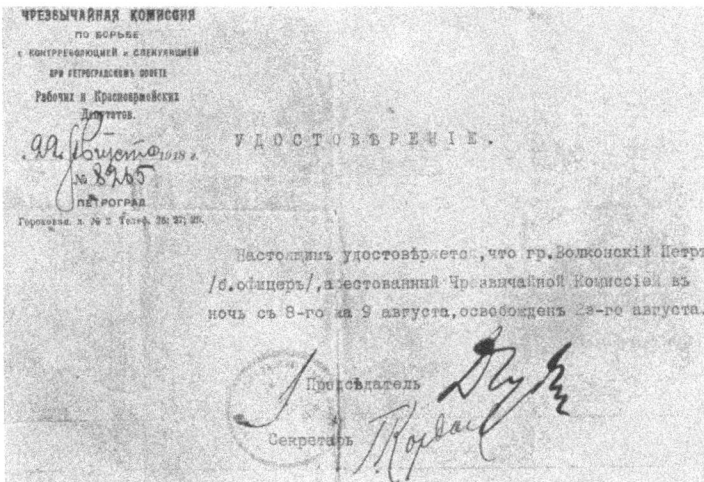

CERTIFICATE OF PIERRE'S FIRST DISMISSAL FROM PRISON IN 1918

Au revoir ; be careful. Many messages to every one !
Hopingly and longingly and lovingly.

P. P. W.

From time to time the return parcel was accompanied by a short poem, written for the most part
in a joking vein. I regret my inability to translate
them into English ; for although the quality of the
verse may not be very high, they show better than
anything else that strength of will that even six months
of a Soviet prison had been unable to impair. All
Pierre's thoughts were for us ; in his letters there
was hardly a word about himself or the hardships
he endured. And, heaven knows, he had grounds
enough for complaint. The sufferings caused by
physical privations were augmented by the deadly
menace for ever hanging over their heads. Nearly
every day some new execution was reported. Nearly
every day the papers published the names of those
who had undergone ' supreme punishment '. Many
of Pierre's cell-companions had been led away never
to return : among them Goudovitch, Sabouroff,
Sasha Dolgoroukoff, and many, many others.
Each time I approached the prison gates I trembled ;
what if I were to hear the terrible answer : ' Wolkonsky is no longer here.' It was a way they had.
Very often they did not tell you straight out :
' We've killed him.' Instead, they talked in riddles :
' He's not here. We know nothing about him.'
Up to you to guess aright.

Many years later I once talked with one of Pierre's prison companions. He personally received no regular food parcels from outside ; only once in a while did his friends send him something. When that happened, when at last the long-awaited parcel reached him, he at once ate everything up ; no matter how big the parcel, he would always finish it the same day, in spite of having to go hungry all the succeeding days. It was not greed that made him act thus. It was the thought that he might be shot that same night and thus lose part of his treasure. The idea was unbearable.

In one of the issues of the Paris magazine *Sovremennyia Zapiski*, Hodasevitch, speaking of the revolutionary poet Essenin, tells us that one of the latter's methods for winning the favours of a girl consisted in promising to show her an execution by the Tcheka. It is quite possible that Essenin was simply boasting. Still, the idea that the death of those dear to us could be considered as an amusement capable of purchasing the caresses of a prostitute is rather upsetting. And yet no attempt has been made on the life of either Trotsky or Stalin, and Dzerjinsky died a natural death !

Prison life had also some comic sides. One day I bought Pierre a piece of soap : a bit of whitish stuff of no particular form wrapped up in a newspaper. Accustomed to all kinds of imitation-food, to substitutes of most unexpected aspect and taste,

Pierre decided this was also something to eat. He
tried it first with salt, then with sugar, put a bit
of it into his tea—it all tasted equally bad. An
Englishman who was imprisoned with Pierre put
him right :

' What are you doing, Prince ? Don't you see—
it's soap ! '

Another day Pierre complained that he suffered
from nervous itching of the skin. The prison
doctor whom he had consulted, had prescribed
bromide and an ointment.

' Are you sure you haven't got any insects ? ' I
asked Pierre.

' I have never seen any.'

The next time I took his dirty linen to the laundry.
I made it undergo a careful inspection. My con-
clusions proved correct : quite a number of lice.
Hardly a case for bromide.

To complete the picture I give here some of my
notes which accompanied the food parcels for
Pierre :

Food Parcel for P. P. Wolkonsky

Kasha, bread, a bottle of milk, cigarettes, have had good
tidings, although uncorroborated, do not lose courage.

Food Parcel for P. P. Wolkonsky, February 11th, 1920.

A pot of kasha (please let me know if better or worse than
usual), bread, milk, cigarettes. Cony has returned ; will

8

try and bring him with me on Sunday. Am trying in vain
to make things move. Don't worry about me. I assure
you that the lack of bread or millet at home contains more
comical than tragical elements. The struggle for life (even
that of others) cannot be really taken quite seriously.

Food Parcel for P. P. Wolkonsky, February 18th, 1920.

A pot of kasha, bread, milk, cigarettes. Salt. Cony is
leaving again. Have written a few words to Grisha.[1] Have
got no good news to communicate. And all my personal
achievements are unfortunately on a plane that has no direct
influence on the actions of the Tcheka.

All my notes were unsigned. I did not believe
I could be mistaken for another.

I had but one thought, one aim in life : the
release of Pierre. Krassin had signed the paper
vouching for Pierre. This document, bearing the
signatures both of Krassin and Gorky was my chief
asset ; the question was now how to use it best.
Elena Nikolaievna came to my rescue. She knew
all and every one in Moscow and had connexions
in the most varied circles. Her plan was soon
ready.

' I am slightly acquainted with the present Commissar of Justice, Krassikoff. I met him before the
Revolution in the house of some friends where he
used to give lessons to the children. If you wish

[1] My brother-in-law, Prince Gregory Wolkonsky, living with his
family in Fall, Esthonia.

I'll ring him up and ask him to come here some day for a cup of tea. Then you will be able to deliver your paper straight into his hands.'

Splendid ! I could wish for no better man than the Commissar of Justice in person. The plan worked smoothly. On the appointed day Krassikoff made his appearance : a big, heavy man, uncouth and grim - looking. . . . Elena Nikolaievna conducted the attack with much diplomatic skill. Krassikoff found himself involved in a general discussion, obliged to defend the Soviet Government. With great heat he started to demonstrate the wisdom and necessity of its latest measures. That was where we had him.

' You speak of justice, but do you know of all that is being done in its name ? To take but one example : the husband of Sofia Alexeevna has been in prison for nearly half a year. No accusation has been made against him ; he has never been brought before a judge, but has simply been notified that he is going to be kept as hostage till the end of the civil war. Such people as Krassin and Gorky are ready to vouch for him, but even they are helpless. The notion of taking hostages is in itself something awful—a dark and terrible custom of the Middle Ages. And you talk of justice ! '

Krassikoff was somewhat taken aback.

' Well, a mistake is always possible. Put down in writing all the essential features of the case and let me have the paper. If things are sa you say, we'll look over the case and see what can be done. The innocent have nothing to fear from us.'

That was the very thing we wanted.   A few days later, having obtained a special pass to the Kremlin, I delivered a detailed statement of Pierre's case at the Commissariat of Justice, together with the precious document in which Krassin, Gorky, and several others testified to Pierre's innocence. The first step had been achieved. All that remained was to await results. The procedure would naturally take more than a few days.

Terrible days—days cold and hungry and empty. How humiliating it is for a grown-up person to dream in his sleep of nothing but sweets and pastry. I had no other dreams at that time.   How humiliating, when offered a cup of tea during a chance visit, to catch oneself anxiously following every movement of the hostess, wondering whether another helping of the heavy, under-baked imitation-cake is going to be offered round.   And to have to exert all one's will-power to keep one's hand from snatching the biggest piece lying on the plate.   Those to whom hunger is unknown will never understand the state of mind of the person who in reading a book is less interested in the hero's adventures than in the description of the meals that are served him.   English novels make bad reading as a rule ; the people eat a great deal ; hearty breakfasts, lunches, afternoon teas and late suppers tease the imagination on nearly every page. French authors are less offensive. They write mostly about love. Scientific data goes to prove that in dogs hunger heightens the sexual appetite. It may be true concerning dogs. As to human beings my experience is quite the contrary, i.e., that hunger very decidedly lowers the sex impulse. What is there left of love when you are tempted to compare the green eyes of the beloved, not to the waves of the sea, but to the green colour of freshly-cooked spinach ; when the sight of the tip of her tongue from behind the teeth evokes the idea, not of kisses, but of a well-served dish of calf's tongue. . . . Detective stories are highly recommended ; nothing like a good murder to make you forget the absence of the dinner-gong. One day I should like to write an essay on the literary value of the classics from the point of view of the hungry.

Once a week in company with Valia Mouravieff I attended the evening lectures of Professor Ilyin on the 'Philosophy of Hegel'. It seems strange we should have been in a mood for philosophy, especially for such an abstract teaching as that of Hegel. Yet the lecture-room was always full to the last seat. The fiery words and emotional power of Ilyin swept away all thought of the miseries of our everyday existences ; the magic of his eloquence turned the intricacies of German philosophy into realities, while the charm of pure intellect elevated us above the sufferings of our poor bodies. I have since forgotten all he taught us. I have forgotten even the names of Hegel's works. But I do not think I will ever forget the sight of that lecture-room, the small crowd of cold, hungry students, nor the rapt expression on their pale, emaciated faces.

In tackling Krassikoff I was still far from having exhausted all possible resources. The more people I got interested in Pierre's case the higher were the chances of final success. Among the many person-alities whose aid I sought (and I have difficulty in recalling now even the names of all those I approached) was also the French Communist Sadoul. I had met him once or twice during the first days of the revolution in the house of some friends. Even such slight acquaintance was sufficient to me in my need. Somehow I discovered his address—in the Obouhovsky Pereoulok : a big courtyard, a few trees covered with snow, a low white house. The door was opened by a maid who asked me to wait in the drawing-room. The interior of a rich *bourgeois* house ; a great many French books on the shelves ; mostly novels. Do Communists read novels ?

Sadoul entered, fat, rosy, and gay. I began by reminding him of our former meetings.

' Mais oui, mais oui, je me souviens parfaite-ment.'

I exposed the reason of my visit, told him of

Pierre—could not he exercise his influence in Communist circles to get Pierre released? Oh, but naturally; he would do everything in his power. He noted my name, the name of the prison, etc.

'Je verrai Kamenev demain et lui parlerai de cette affaire.'

'Comment vous remercier!'

'Mais de rien, de rien.'

What a charming man! Why hadn't I thought of coming to him earlier. We talked amiably for another quarter of an hour. Before leaving I asked him to lend me some of his books—I could see he had there a whole library; whilst I was greatly suffering from the absence of anything to read.

'Naturellement, prenez tout ce que vous voulez.'

No one could have been kinder. Enthusiastically I began looking over the titles: this one would do, and this one, and this. . . . His next words arrested me in my task: I could take all I wanted—the books did not really belong to him at all. I understood: a confiscated house, the real owners either shot or in prison. . . . I put back the books I had chosen.

'Thank you so much, but I think I'd better take the books some other time. To-day is not quite convenient.'

I do not know whether he ever talked to Kamenev, as he promised. Quite possibly he did. Kamenev was scarcely interested. As regards Pierre's fate the practical results were nil.

From time to time numbers of the former *bourgeois* class were called upon to work for the community. These tasks had nothing to do with the duty of keeping clean the part of the street and pavement opposite their own house, which fell to the lot of all the inhabitants of the city. Once or twice a week all the lodgers, with the exception of the very old and feeble, were turned out into the street and supplied with crowbars, shovels, brooms, etc. We did our work conscientiously : broke up the ice, shovelled the snow into big heaps, swept the pavement. Nobody thought of complaining ; the work had to be done and we were quite ready to do our part.

The forced labour for the *bourgeoisie* was a very different thing. One day I received a summons— an order, under severe penalty, to present myself at eight o'clock next morning at the meeting place in a former police station.

I started at half-past seven. It was a dreary December morning, dark and cold ; the snow was falling in big, heavy flakes, and I had had no breakfast. The room in the police station was unheated. We were about forty : young girls, ladies in old-fashioned hats, some in evening shoes and darned silk stockings ; old gentlemen in worn overcoats, with pale faces and dull eyes. . . . A motley crowd. . . .

We had to wait for more than half an hour : shivering, sleepy, miserable. At last they made

their appearance : well-fed, brutal, self-satisfied.
First they counted us and marked the names of
those absent. Then a column was formed, the
order given, the march started. Across the whole
town. Like prisoners, surrounded by an armed
guard we were conveyed to the Riazansky station,
situated at the other end of Moscow—a good hour's
march. We were exhausted when we reached our
destination. There they divided us into groups,
and each group was given a separate task. It fell
to my lot, with five or six others, to clean the snow
from an empty space behind the station. They
gave us big, heavy wooden shovels. The soldiers
of our guard seated themselves round, lighted their
cigarettes, and prepared to enjoy the show. It
was quite evident that the task given us was a useless
and unnecessary one ; that its only point lay in
humiliating us, the formerly privileged, in making
us feel more keenly the cruel hand of to-day's
masters and our own helplessness. The soldiers
encouraged us mockingly in our work, laughing
loudly at their own silly jokes. ' Eh, you citizen-
ness ! you needn't be afraid of a bit of snow. High
time you learn to do something with your hands.
Hurry up ! ' The girl turned a wan face towards
her tormentors. The heavy shovel with its load of
snow seemed quite above the forces of that slender
figure and the tiny delicate hands. She was going
to say something when her foot in its ridiculous
high-heeled shoe slipped, gave way, and landed her

on all fours, up to the waist in the snow. Loud
guffaws greeted her misadventure : ' That's a good
one. Worthy of the circus ! Skirts just a bit
higher, please ! Ho ! ho ! ho ! ' Not a hand
stretched out to help her. . . . A little farther on an
old man, even more poorly dressed than the rest,
stood leaning against the wall. The pouches under
the eyes, the grey pallor of the skin, all spoke of
some serious disease. "Hello, Grandpa ! What do
you imagine you're here for ? All your life long
you have rested, now it is your turn to work while
we look on.' The leering faces were full of low
vindictiveness. What a joy to be able to order
about those one had always had to obey ! There
is no sight so ugly as the human beast in its moments
of triumph.

In most situations in life many different emotions
are combined. Here there was only one feeling, on
their side as well as on ours : the feeling of hatred,
in its purest and most intense form. ' *In statu
nascendi*,' say the chemists.

At dusk they dismissed us. By way of reward,
each of us got a pound of the usual damp, clammy
black bread, baked with bits of straw and even
tree bark in it. Silently we made our way home,
exhausted physically, morally humiliated and degraded. Thus did the victorious proletariat build
up a new world.

Two or three weeks later we got another summons.
Every apartment in the house was to send forth

two of its members to clean the lavatories and
water-closets in various communal and Government
buildings. Which of us would go ? . . . I refused.
Let them put me in prison, let them shoot me, or do
anything they liked—I was not going to submit. . . .

' And if no one goes ? '

' I do not know and I do not care. I tell you,
whatever happens, nobody is going to force me to
clean other peoples' W.C.s ' . . .

I stayed at home. And nothing happened. At
the appointed hour the required number of workers
made their appearance. Trotsky is supposed to
have said : ' Put up a notice that on such a day a
general flogging is going to take place, and all the
bourgeois will obediently form a queue.'

Worst of all, perhaps, were the night searches.
On ordinary days the electric current was cut off
in the whole town at about nine p.m. If the light
kept on burning in a certain district after that hour
it meant that the Tcheka intended visiting one of the
houses. The people dared not go to bed, and sat
trembling in fearful anticipation, listening to the
sound of the rare motor-cars that passed in the
street below ; at once all conversation ceased, all
thoughts were fixed on the one question—would it
stop at the door, or would it pass on ? No one
but Tchekists used a motor-car by night. They
usually arrived about two in the morning : a loud
knocking at the door, loud, impatient voices on the

landing, heavy footsteps, the thud of rifles, and the
irruption of a dozen or so Red soldiers, uncere-
moniously taking possession of the whole flat.   Then
hour after hour of the search : everything turned
upside down, drawers forced open, their contents
spread out on the table or thrown on to the floor,
every single thing minutely examined. . . . Strange
hands rummaging among your dresses, crumpling
up your linen ; enemy eyes reading your correspondence ; all your most intimate belongings looked
over, discussed by a hostile crowd. . . . The first
grey light of dawn showing up a picture of utter
confusion and desolation.   And lastly the most
critical moment of all : the departure.   Would
anybody be arrested ?   It has all been depicted
many times.   All who lived in Russia during those
years know the suspense of those terrible nights.
Nobody escaped.   Even to-day I hate the sound of
a motor-car stopping at my door late in the evening.

We were lucky.   They visited us twice that
winter, but departed without making any arrests.

Many years later I was staying with some friends
in Paris.   I had gone to bed early and was asleep
when my hostess, just back from the theatre, knocked
at my door.   In one second I was out of bed :
'What's the matter ? Have they come for a
search ? ' . . . A kind of conditional reflex that
takes a long time to disappear.

I lived from Sunday to Sunday, for the short

minutes I was allowed to be with Pierre. On Saturday I would begin cooking the food and getting things ready. The most difficult part was in taking the food to the camp. The parcel was very heavy, while the distance made a good hour's walk. Lisette would help me to dress : warm underwear, my fur coat, then the heavy pot of kasha that she strapped behind my shoulders ; in one hand the bottle of milk, in another the bag. Slowly, step by step, like a pack-donkey I made my way. It was essential to arrive at least an hour in advance. The visiting time was from one to three ; visitors were let in by groups of twenty for a quarter of an hour's interview. After three o'clock no more visitors were admitted. It often happened that the last comers were not allowed in. To be on the safe side, one had to take one's place in the queue an hour or even two in advance. Then stand in the snow and wait ; if you went away for even a few minutes you risked losing your place. There were days that winter when the mercury fell as low as twenty and more degrees below zero.[1] It was torture. Week after week I stood in that queue ; on all the faces one could read an expression of dull misery ; that of sleepers in the grip of some terrible nightmare : faces of generals who had become street-vendors, pampered society ladies who had been turned into washerwomen. The new-comers could be recognized by their nervousness, by the

[1] — $20°$ Réamur$= - 25°$ Celsius $= - 13°$ Fahrenheit.

poignant anxiety in their eyes ; the blow smashing their lives had only just fallen and they had not yet had time to adjust themselves to the new conditions. During periods of political unrest the queue before the prison gates grew longer ; in times of quiet, shorter : a kind of thermometer by which one could judge the degree of nervousness pervading Government circles.

When the time for our interview came, I was usually on the verge of collapse from cold and weariness. One got but little joy from those hasty fifteen minutes, among a crowd of strangers, under the ever-vigilant eyes of the prison guard. My mind would be a blank : the words I had been thinking over the whole week were forgotten, the tenderness that filled the heart remained unspoken. A hurried kiss, a few broken sentences—the meeting was over.

A source of acute misery for Pierre lay in his inability to help his mother. Her letters were tragic :

'. . . My life is becoming unbearable,' wrote Mother-in-law in a post card of 1/14 December 1919, ' especially because of my staff, who are all without exception brutal. As I told Sophy, I am simply afraid of remaining here by myself, so tell me what I am to do. . . . Je crains de succomber si cela dure. I beg you for an answer and for advice. Up to now I did not want to tell you all this. On me tire les cheveux, me bat et me pousse comme on ne le ferait pas avec un chien, c'est hystérique peut-être, mais c'est horrible. Pardon et supplie réponds.[1] God protect you and all of us. The old man is like the rest and cunning. Forgive me.

MAMA.

And here is a post card from the 22 December, old style, a few days before Christmas, written in very fine handwriting, and hardly readable in parts :

DIMANCHE SOIR

December 22nd—January 4th, 1919/20.

' Glory to God in Heaven and peace on earth, and good will among the people. Christ is born, Christ our God ; the Angels sing in Heaven and let us on earth sing God's glory in eternity.'

My dearest, I am alive and go on existing in the hope of seeing you, but I am not well and suffer greatly. I have pains in my whole body, I think it comes from rheumatism. I am hungry and very cold. I hope you and Sophy will soon give me some good news, and that you will take me under your roof. I am incapable of doing anything ; loneliness and pain have broken my spirit, while the staff is only waiting de se débarasser de moi. Perche demande un espèce de testament, et la petite dit que certainement cela serait heureux que je disparaisse puisque je suis assez vieille. Tout cela on me le dit à moi. Le vieux est grossier au delà de toute expression, que le bon Dieu le leur pardonne, ils ne savent ce qu'ils font. . . . Ecrivez moi et consolez moi, il y a si longtemps que tu ne m'as pas écrit,

---

[1] ' I am afraid of giving way if this continues. . . . They pull my hair, beat me and push me, in a way one would not treat a dog. It is perhaps hysterical but it is horrible. Forgive me and answer, I implore you . . .'

les dernières nouvelles étaient de Sophy du 15/28 et de
Lisette du 17/30. Que Dieu vous garde ainsi que nous
tous. Je bénis et j'embrasse toi et Sophy tendrement.
J'implore des nouvelles.[1]

I would not wish my worst enemy ever to receive
such a letter from his mother. What could we do ?
She asked Pierre for shelter, and he was locked up in
prison. She turned for help to us who suffered
even more than she did from cold and hunger. It
was the knowledge of his utter helplessness that
made Pierre suffer most.

Christmas came, then New Year. . . . Had Krassikoff forgotten me ?

No, he kept his word. One day, in the middle
of January, I received an official paper informing
me that at the last sitting of the V.C.I.K.[2] the case
of citizen Pierre Wolkonsky had been examined and
the decision taken ' to propose to the Vetcheka
to liberate citizen Wolkonsky.' Hurrah ! Hurrah !
Hurrah ! Never had I felt so happy. I jumped, I

---

[1] ' . . . The staff is only waiting to get rid of me. Perche insists on
my making some kind of will, and the girl says that it would certainly be
a good thing if I were to disappear as I am quite old enough. All this
is said to my face. The old man is rude beyond description—may God
forgive them for they know not what they do. Write and console me ;
it is so long since you last wrote ; the latest news was from Sophy from
the 15/28, and from Lisette from the 17/30. May God protect you as
well as all of us. I bless and embrace you and Sophy tenderly. I beg
for news.'

[2] V.C.I.K.=The All-Russian Central Executive Committee, which
according to the Constitution represented the highest authority in the
country.

danced, I was ready to embrace the whole world.   I
could hardly keep still, kept rushing from one room
to the other, telling everybody : ' Have you heard ?
They are going to release Pierre ! '   In my delight
I paid scarcely any attention to the somewhat
ambiguous form of the resolution.   Why ' propose '
to the Tcheka ?   Why not simply order that he
should be liberated.   However, the V.C.I.K. was
the highest power in the land.   Its decisions were
supreme.   There was surely no reason to worry.

A day passed, then another and another. Nothing
happened. What could it mean ? Why hadn't he been
set free ?   I decided to go and inquire at the Tcheka.

' When will Wolkonsky be let out of prison ? '

' We know nothing about it.'

' How can that be ?   It is a decision of the
V.C.I.K. ! '

' That does not concern us.'

I could not believe my ears.   The Tcheka was
officially subordinated to the V.C.I.K. ; it could not
possibly ignore the resolution of the centre.   I was
wrong : it not only could but most decidedly did
so.   Day after day passed, and I was forced to come
to the evident conclusion : the Tcheka had no
intention of letting Pierre go.   From the pinnacle
of happiness fate had once more sent me spinning
into an abyss of misery.

I had to start all over again from the beginning.
I sought out Krassikoff and Krassin, interviewed

9

Enoukidze, the secretary of the V.C.I.K., then Kamenev, Kalinin, etc. . . . . They shrugged their shoulders. What else could they do ? The Tcheka had infinitely more power than each one of them separately and all of them put together.

In the Communist party itself voices were being raised against the unlimited power of the Tcheka. At the beginning of February a new decree was issued : executions would now be carried out only after a regular trial. The decree was printed in the papers and was posted all over the town. I can still see the corner of the street where I stopped and read it first. A terrible load was lifted from my shoulders. Somebody next to me was making the sign of the cross. . . . Now at last I would be able to sleep quietly.

How naïve we were ! Would we never understand the real nature of our adversary ? It should have been easy to guess that all those fine promises meant nothing, that the Tcheka would continue its secret executions in exactly the same way as it had always done ; as it has done ever since until to-day. The only effect of the decree was a series of summary executions ordered by the Tcheka the night before the publication of the decree. Many perished that night—some said many dozens, some said many hundreds . . .

The day following the decree Pierre wrote me by ' return parcel ' :

After yesterday's removal of the sword of Damocles, people in my situation are no longer of even the slightest interest. Isn't it strange that it should have happened yesterday, while only the day before I had asked you to pray for me. Now, I can wish all those dear to me, and you above all—one thing only : to leave, to leave, to leave—in the knowledge that I remain here full of gratitude and without losing hope for the future.

P. P. W.

Very fine phrases. . . . Yet he must have known quite well that no power on earth could make me go away leaving him all alone in a Bolshevik prison !

Towards the middle of February we learnt from the Soviet newspapers of the tragic end of Admiral Kolchak ; and of how a French general sanctioned the delivery of the commander of an Allied Army into the hands of the enemy—delivery that meant certain death to the defeated admiral, who had been taken under the official protection of the colours of all the Allied Powers. Russians will be slow to forget the name of General Janin.

Some one advised me to go and see Mrs. Peshkoff. She could have hardly received me less cordially : a hard, dry voice, a few cold insignificant words ; the lady herself—a tall, black figure, very thin, very distant, very indifferent. How strange it was to think that she was the first wife of Gorky. And now sad that she should be at the head of the

Political Red Cross in aid of prisoners. It was later explained to me that the Political Red Cross was in the hands of Socialists and was only interested in prisoners of advanced political opinions. The fate of a 'former prince' did not concern them in the least.

Once a year the Political Red Cross in Paris organizes a charity entertainment among the Russian refugees. I naturally never go there. Unfortunately I have no other way of expressing my resentment.

Once again I decided to try and tackle Enoukidze, the secretary of the V.C.I.K. The first difficulty lay in getting a pass to the Kremlin. There were several ways of obtaining one, but the time has not yet come to disclose certain things. Those who helped us are still there and could be made to suffer. The point is—I obtained the pass and saw Enoukidze.

' Can you tell me why, contrary to the decision of the V.C.I.K., Wolkonsky is still in prison ? '

He did not deny the facts. Promised me they would not leave it at that, but would insist on the Tcheka taking their decision into account ! Words . . . words. . . .

Serge said he would talk to the Commissar Lounatcharsky, Cony Benckendorff promised to see Vorovsky. Still another friend promised to see some one else.

One evening M. dropped in to see me. He had joined the Bolsheviks and was now working with them, honestly believing it to be the best way of serving his country.

' If your husband were to agree to enter the Commissariat of Foreign Affairs and work for the Bolsheviks, he would be set free immediately.'

' I feel sure he will not agree.'

At my next meeting with Pierre I repeated to him the conversation. He burst out laughing. I had not expected anything else. I knew he still believed in the strength of the ancient formula *noblesse oblige.*

A new misery was in store for us ; it came in the form of a notice from the ' house committee ' telling us to be ready to receive two new lodgers into our flat. We were, it appeared, occupying more space than was allotted us according to Soviet law. Re-criminations were of no avail. The couple thus forced on us—a young man and his wife—seemed quite nice, but . . . they were Communists. Even before their arrival there was none too much space in that flat. The Communists living in the next room were like the famous pea under the mattress that keeps one from sleeping all night ; like the bit of dust in one's eye that after hours of vain rubbing feels like that beam which, according to tradition, one ought to remark only when it is in the eye of one's neighbour. Nothing could be more

disagreeable than this living in close contact (having
to cook our dinners on the same stove, to use the
same bathroom devoid of hot water, etc.), with
people who considered themselves *a priori* and in
principle as our foes. Nothing could be more
irritating than the feeling of being, even at home,
under the constant eye of the enemy. ' Take care ',
' Shut the door ', ' Do not talk so loud ; the Communists may hear you '. Pin-pricks ? Yes, of
course. But in that nightmare life of ours every
pin-prick took the proportion of a serious wound.

I was beginning to despair. All ways had been
tried, all protection sought, all connexions appealed
to. All of no avail. Pierre was in prison and the
chances of his being set free seemed to grow less
and less with every day. The Tcheka having refused
to obey the decision of the V.C.I.K., the case was to
all appearances lost. Nothing remained but to wait
for a universal revolution with general pardon to all
political prisoners ; pending which I could see but
one last move to be made.

At that time a peace treaty had just been signed
between Soviet Russia and Esthonia, according to
which the subjects of both countries were to be
allowed to return unmolested to their native land.
Several generations of the Wolkonsky family had
owned land near Reval, and all the members of the
family, as belonging to the nobility of the former
province of Esthonia, had full right to consider

themselves Esthonian Nationals. If the Soviet
Government gave us permission to return to Reval
—and there could be no official reason for refusing
it—then Pierre would automatically be released.
My brother-in-law would be able to conduct all
the Esthonian part of the transaction from Fall.
The chief drawback to this plan consisted in the
length of time it would take. Even with the best of
luck many months would inevitably elapse before
any result was attained. That meant weeks and
weeks more of prison for Pierre. And there was
always the possibility of failure in the end.

One more worry was now added to the rest.
And a most essential one—the money question. A
short time after my arrival in Moscow a letter came
from Petrograd with the news that my flat on the
English Quay had been seized by a party of sailors.
Protests proved fruitless. All my belongings, the
furniture, the books, the linen, everything had been
taken. . . . All the little things one loves, all my
souvenirs, all my private letters. . . . Why had I
been so stupid as to rely on the protection of that
paper of Eses's. How could I have placed any
confidence in the signature of a man like Lenin ?

Life has a logic of its own ; it may forgive us
our sins, may leave unpunished our blackest crimes
. . . but never will fate pardon an act of stupidity,
it will make us pay unmercifully, over and over
again for every trifling mistake.

I regretted the things lost not only because of

their sentimental value. What hurt me most was the thought of the many months I would have been able to keep both Pierre and myself by selling the contents of the flat. Whereas now, thanks to my own mistake, we were reduced to misery. . . . The signature of Lenin, indeed !

My money was coming to an end. I could see no hope of Pierre ever being released. . . .

One day I was returning from prison in a very black mood, when in the street I met Count Paul X.

' How are you getting on ? ' he asked.

' Badly, very badly.'

' And Pierre ? '

' In prison.'

' Have you been to see Bogouslavsky ? '

' No, I've never heard of him before.'

Paul explained, talking as usual in his quick, exuberant way, excitedly gesticulating. Bogouslavsky, said he, is a very mysterious personage, an old ' sea-dog ', who has many connexions with the Tcheka, is even said to be a personal friend of the all-powerful Dzerjinsky ; at the same time Bogouslavsky never refuses his help to the victims of the Soviet régime and has already saved many of them from prison. Paul was going to see him in the immediate future ; if I wished, he could talk to him about Pierre.

' Be a dear and do it ! I'll be grateful to you all my life if only you get Pierre out of prison.'

He jotted down the chief points of the case.

' I cannot, of course, promise you anything.   But I will do my best.'

He warned me it would probably entail certain expenses.   That did not frighten me.   I knew not in what way, but the money would be forthcoming.

I have forgotten to mention one small fact, which, however ridiculous in itself, presented one more difficulty in the way of Pierre's liberation.   It took place just after his arrest.   During the roll-call his name was shouted : ' Wolkonsky ! ' ' Present.' ' Prince ? ' ' Yes, with the title of Serene Highness.'   They were much impressed by the grandness of this title ; it became in their eyes one more argument for keeping him in prison.   The pleasure of a fine gesture had to be dearly expiated.

Some time ago, in Paris, I met Prince N., who had been imprisoned at the same time as Pierre.   He told me the story of his arrest.   ' When I was taken to be examined, the first question was : " You are Prince N. ? "   I replied : " The name is right, but I am no prince.   Of noble birth—yes, but no prince."   That answer saved me ; to the end they remained under doubt as to whether I was a prince or not.   Otherwise I would probably even now be in prison.'

It is curious to note how in a similar situation two people will react in practically opposite ways.

Of course Prince N. was a thousand times right. There is no shame in resorting to a ruse when dealing with a relentless foe out to destroy you. But I cannot imagine the circumstances that could force Pierre to disavow the name of his forefathers. No, not even to save his life. An extraordinary lack of adaptability.

My visits to the prison were becoming more and more sad. Pierre knew I had done everything in my power, and that all my plans had failed. My notes that accompanied the food parcels reflect this despairing mood. Here is a note on February 22nd 1920 :

Please forgive the inferior quality of to-day's provisions : a pot of kasha, unfortunately not thick enough, a bottle of milk, a piece of bread, and, alas ! a packet of makhorka.[1] No good news. Don't you think it would be a wise plan for you to give me a letter to your mother on Sunday, asking her to send me her Esthonian papers, (I will find some way for her to do it), and also yours if Sepper can find them ? You could at the same time write a few words to Grisha. All that is happening to us now is only a test of the theory that ' all these things are of no importance.' And it is important that theory should conquer. I have sometimes got the feeling that you are not you and that I am not I.

Our one hope was now based on the Esthonian

[1] The very inferior tobacco smoked by the people. Up till then I had always managed to supply Pierre with cigarettes.

treaty—a remote and highly questionable affair ; but there was no other way. For the present there was nothing before us but prison—prison and prison. . . . With brave words we tried to keep up each other's courage, but in our hearts we were near to despair.

There exists a theory called the Lange-James's theory on the origin of emotions. According to these two learned scientists our emotions are only the subjective states that accompany certain physical reactions, and are only the consequences and not the reasons producing these manifestations. Thus, we cry not because we are sad, but we are sad because we cry. No doubt in certain cases by forcing yourself to laugh you can to some extent dispel your black mood. But I would have liked to see either Lange or James in my place in the early spring of 1920 ; I am sure they would have modified their theory.

I had to acknowledge myself defeated.

And then, quite unexpectedly, the impossible happened. On Wednesday, the 25th of February, I had brought my parcel of provisions to the prison gates. After delivering it into the hands of the guard, I stood waiting for the usual ' return parcel '.

Suddenly, from behind the gates came the voice of Pierre : ' I am free ! '

' What ? What are you saying ? '

' Yes, I have already been notified.'

' Then why do you not come out at once ? '

' There is no hurry. I've got my things to pack ;
then I want to take leave of my companions. Come
back here at two and bring with you the little
sledge for my box.'

I cannot to this day understand how a man who
had been kept in prison (and what a prison !) for
nearly nine months did not take the very first
opportunity to leave the prison gates behind him :
and especially under Bolshevik rule, when every
moment a change might have taken place, the order
have been revoked and liberty refused. This small
detail reflects the whole character of Pierre. It was
one of the things that astonished me most in the
course of the whole Revolution.

A quarter to two found me once more before the
prison gates. It was a clear, cold day. The snow
on the roofs glittered in the sun, whilst the first
uncertain signs of coming spring already filled the
air. Never before had the sun shone so brightly,
never had the birds sung so triumphantly. . . . All
nature was rejoicing with me. This was a day of
days. Such a day could never be repeated !

Punctually, at the stroke of two, the gates flew
open and Pierre came out. Kotzebue, a friend of
long standing, helped us to fasten the things on to
the sledge. Pierre was leaving, whereas he was
remaining in prison.

In 1925, in the courtyard of the Russian church in the rue Daru in Paris, somebody called my name. I turned round. It was Kotzebue. 'Do you remember?' 'Do you remember!'

CHAPTER IV

PIERRE was now free. To begin with—home and a bath.

After a short rest—he had really earned it with his nine months in a Soviet prison—Pierre went to see and thank all those who in one way or another had tried to help him regain his freedom. One of his first visits was to Bogouslavsky. Pierre had hardly opened his mouth when the latter interrupted him :

' Do not thank any one. You owe your freedom entirely to your wife.'

' How is that ? '

In answer Bogouslavsky told Pierre how he had obtained his release. When Count Paul X had asked him to help us, Bogouslavsky appealed to Dzerjinsky.

' Felix Edouardovitch,' said he, ' have you ever read Nekrassof ? '

' I know, I know,' interrupted Dzerjinsky. ' You want to speak of " Russian Women " and of the Princess Wolkonsky,' [1] and he immediately signed an order for Pierre's release.

That is what Bogouslavsky told Pierre. It is, all

[1] See footnote on page 109.

modesty apart, a most remarkable story ; probably
a true one—there was no reason why Bogouslavsky
should have invented it. We do not, as a rule
credit Tchekists with such gentlemanly feelings ;
we hardly picture them otherwise than as complete
villains, incapable of any human emotions. Is it
possible that even a Dzerjinsky had his moments of
weakness ?

We will probably never learn the answer. Bogouslavsky has since been shot and Dzerjinsky died of
heart-failure.

When at present I sometimes nag Pierre with a
trifling request which he is unwilling to grant (and
is there a wife who never exasperates her own
husband ?), he exclaims : ' This is moral black-
mail. She has saved me out of a Bolshevik prison
and knows that I cannot refuse her anything ! '

Pierre was now free. Our next task was to get
safely out of the country. We knew that to go
abroad meant to condemn ourselves to a long
period of exile ; possibly for the rest of our lives.
But we had no choice. You cannot live under a
Government that regards you as an enemy and treats
you as a criminal. We had been bereft of everything.
Most of us were ready to forget the past and start
life anew. But we could not go over to those who
adopted murder, tyranny, and oppression as a means
of ruling the country. Good upbringing is in many
ways a handicap ; traditions that have been handed

down for generations can only be forgotten with
great difficulty and after many years. How could
we join the ranks of those for whom the word
' gentleman ' was a term of abuse ?

Had Pierre and I been alone we would certainly
have found some way of leaving the country. There
always are people willing to help you secretly across
the frontier in return for a reward. Of course there
were risks : the frontier was well guarded, and
there was, besides, a considerable danger of
falling into the hands of a traitor, who, having
received the price of your passage, delivered you
straight into the hands of the Tcheka. Quite a
number of our friends and acquaintances got
caught : among others the Golitsins, the Fehleisens,
the Ermoloffs. The latter's failure was due entirely
to their own carelessness. They were attempting
to escape under assumed names, with false documents and faked passports. Part of the journey
was to be made by railway. When their luggage
was opened at the station for the usual inspection,
a little box with old visiting-cards fell out : cards
with Ermoloff's real name and court title—' Cham-
bellan de sa Majesté '. Denial was useless and
both husband and wife were sent to finish their
journey in prison.[1]

However, these adventurous ways of escape were

[1] Such was the story told to me. I cannot, of course, vouch for its
accuracy.

not for us ; we could neither force my mother-in-law to travel in a jolting peasant cart nor dress her up as a Finnish milkmaid. There could be no question of her covering several miles on foot through woods and marshes when she could scarcely move unaided from one room to another. The only course open to us was to obtain legal permission to leave Russia as Esthonian nationals.

My mother-in-law's letters were becoming more and more desperate, and were a source of ever-growing anxiety to us. Pierre's one desire was to go to Petrograd and to see what could be done to help her.

We were now faced with the difficulty of obtaining railway fares to Petrograd. Here again Bogouslavsky came to the rescue.

' I will send you on an official mission to Petrograd as lecturer of the Balt-Flot University. I will myself write out the certificate.'

' But . . . no such university exists ! '

' That does not matter.'

' What if the control officer questions me ? '

' Just tell them that the university is situated in the Starokonioushenny Pereoulok,' and Bogouslavsky named the number of the house and flat he himself occupied.

A big lie is often safer than a small one. One could have suspected us of inventing a fictitious appointment, but no one would believe that we

10

had invented a whole university.   The safety of the falsehood lay in its enormity.

I was sad to leave Moscow.   A winter together in Soviet Russia binds people more than a world flight in the ' Graf Zeppelin '.

We were the first of our little group to leave. Six months later all the others had likewise gone their way.   Only old Nadejda Amandovna remained in the flat, like a faithful watchdog guarding the property of the long-forgotten owner.   Serge and Elena Nikolaievna went abroad ; Olga entered the Petrograd School of Art ; whilst Lisette—beautiful, proud Lisette—broke with her family and married (according to Soviet law) a spiteful little Communist Jew.

Every marriage is a jump into the unknown.   It all depends on the quality of your parachute.   The cautious do not rely on passion alone to land them safely.

A few weeks later, in Petrograd, Lisette visited us with her husband.   She was very much in love.

' Just imagine,' said she, ' when he thinks of the past and of the humiliating restrictions against the Jews that existed under the old régime, he actually trembles with rage.'

(The difficulty of the Jewish question consists, according to Pierre, in the impossibility of putting a cross over it.)

Has Lisette found happiness ?   I do not know.

When she was in Paris, three years ago, she did not come to see us. Did she want to avoid in her new life all reminder of the past, all that could possibly reopen old wounds ? Did she fear we would misunderstand her ? Or did the sightseeing and shopping in Paris leave her no time to come all the way to Clichy ? Who knows ? Next time you are in Paris, Lisette, you will perhaps come and see us ?

Our journey from Moscow to Petrograd was accomplished in the best possible conditions. Aniouta Obolensky,[1] who was travelling by the same train, had succeeded, by some ruse, in capturing the heart of one of the high Soviet officials, and had thus obtained a whole compartment to herself in a car which formerly belonged to the International Sleeping-car Company. She very kindly gave me the lower berth, while Pierre slept on the floor.

Our chief difficulty lay in passing the barrier at the Petrograd station. Would the suspicion of the official in control be roused at the sight of Pierre's certificate ? The art of bluff lies in knowing how to control one's features. But what are the emotions of the poker-table compared to this !

It may have been my face, it may have been the paper itself, but the official smelt a rat. At the same time he was afraid of showing his ignorance.

[1] Daughter of Prince Alexis Obolensky, former Procurator of the Holy Synod.

So they let us pass, with a ' Take care, if your papers prove false, we'll get you yet ! ' This threat cost me a whole box of sleeping-powders.

Petrograd. How strange it felt being in one's native city and having nowhere to go. My mother-in-law's house on the Fourstadtskaia, where we had lived with Pierre last winter, was occupied by the Bashkirs ; my flat—by a group of Red sailors ; my father's house on the Galernaia had been turned into a museum ; my mother's apartments had been plundered. . . . We could have perhaps insisted on some room being allotted us in one of the houses. But—one of the first rules of safety during social revolutions is to avoid attracting the attention of the authorities, as long as they do not actually molest you. Prison is always ready to receive such as us. I sincerely hope that my English readers will be able to profit by my experience—should their turn come.

A well-known authoress [1] helped us out of the difficulty. In pre-revolutionary days (could it really have been but three years ago ?) she had once stayed at my flat for a certain time. Now that we were rendered homeless, she kindly offered us the room that had been set apart for her in the so-called ' Home of Arts ', and for which she had no use herself. We were quick to accept this offer.

The Home of Arts was situated on the Moika, in the house that in pre-revolutionary days belonged

[1] Avoid all names is another important rule of the revolutionary game.

MY FATHER'S HOUSE IN ST. PETERSBURG

(COURT SIDE)

to a rich merchant called Elisseeff. It had now been turned into an abode for homeless writers, artists, and poets : Andrei Biely, Tchoukovsky, Volynsky, Piast—all these names mean nothing to the great British Public, but are more or less familiar to every educated Russian.

The room they gave us was on the third floor—the study of the former owner. On the walls were still hanging photographs of his family, gentlemen and ladies in old-fashioned dresses, with that fixed, unnatural smile usually seen only on the faces of kings in the accomplishment of their duties, and on that of newly married couples waiting for the train to start. Next door to the study was a vast toilet room, with various appliances for physical training. We could have found nothing more suitable ; rooms in a Soviet Home constituted *an und für sich*, a strong protection against ever possible mishap.

We found Mother-in-law in a very sad state. The hardships of the winter, added to the misery of constant loneliness, had undermined her both in health and spirit. Nothing remained now of the once-famous beauty, rich, spoilt, and flattered by all those surrounding her. We had before us an old woman, half-deaf, ailing in body, suffering from very pronounced oedema of the legs, as the result of constant under-feeding. Thus we saw with our own eyes how people actually swell from hunger. She had so little strength left that most of the time she remained in bed. Her mind had also lost much of its former alertness, and she grasped but vaguely the great changes that were taking place all round her. It was perhaps better so ; the contrast was too great between those last two years of her life and the seventy preceding. She would not, or could not, admit the fact that all her splendid jewels—her famous pearls, her diamond necklace, etc., were irretrievably lost ; she clung to the childish illusion that those men in black leather jackets who had come one night and taken away all her treasures were secretly acting in her own interest, and were somewhere keeping guard over her jewels.

' On m'a dit qu'ils ont mis tout ça dans un endroit sûr.'

We said nothing. In some cases the human organism protects itself against the blows of life by sacrificing the clearness of its brain ; amnesia, delirium, madness are but so many devices of a mind unable to face the horrors of reality.

Poor Mother-in-law ! In a voice trembling from feebleness and old age, she poured forth her childish futile complaints : she was all alone, every one had forsaken her, the maid Mathilda hurt her when dressing her hair. . . . But sometimes the old spirit of authority would return ; she no longer complained, she demanded . . . and all Pierre's pleading, backed up by the skill of long diplomatic training, hardly sufficed to calm her.

PRINCESS VERA WOLKONSKY

MY LATE MOTHER-IN-LAW, AT THE AGE OF SIXTY-FIVE,
IN COURT DRESS (1913)

But no matter how strong her bodily sufferings, no matter how great the privations endured, never once did she lose faith in the wisdom and mercy of Divine Providence. She continued reading, with failing eyesight, the daily chapter from the Holy Scriptures ; never once did she omit to recite her prayers, devoutly kneeling—when her strength permitted—on the floor before the ikons. And up to the end she kept telling us : ' Il faut croire en la Miséricorde de Dieu ! '

To begin with, we lived on what we managed to get by selling a few of my old sheets, that had, in our pre-revolutionary incarnation, formed part of my trousseau. (I quite consciously use this somewhat exaggerated term ; it seems hardly possible that in this same life we should have once belonged to that class of people who get rich dowries, ask empresses to their weddings and have music at their funerals.)

Nowhere in the world do women cherish their fine linen so much as in France. A short time ago we were staying at a rich estate in northern France. When I saw the love with which the lady of the house attended personally to the heaps of napkins sheets, towels, etc., that had once belonged to her forefathers, I could not help comparing it to the careless indifference with which we had always abandoned our linen to the care of some hired maid or housekeeper. Inanimate things have a way of avenging themselves. I understood this when on my way to sell those miserable half-dozen sheets, which were all that remained of our former riches. Each single sheet represented several days' existence for Pierre and myself.

Our money flew with a speed that would have undoubtedly beaten all the records in the world. . . . The sheets were all gone, and I kept awake at nights wondering whether death from starvation would overtake us next week or the week after. Rescue came in an unexpected form : Aniouta Obolensky had in some way discovered that the Board of the Soviet Library Committee included a few very kind gentlemen. They were ready, if asked, to effect a fictitious requisition of your library, and help you to get it out of your confiscated house. You thus acquired the possibility of selling your own books, for by some unexplained whim of the authorities a few bookshops in Petrograd had been left open. It would have been fruitless to look for logic in the behaviour of our new masters, but we could sometimes profit by its absence.

Aniouta's information proved correct. I will not attempt to describe my feelings when Pierre and myself, acting as assistants to a bright little Jew from the Library Committee, entered my lovely flat on the English Quay. I am not what is usually called a sentimentalist. But to witness my own rooms occupied by strangers, to see uncouth sailors

making themselves at home among my things, eating
off my china, sleeping in my bed, on my own sheets
. . . no, I never thought it would be quite as
unpleasant.   Our sense of property has been developed in us for generations ; the inverse process
will probably take as long—if not longer.

I've got to acknowledge that the intruders had kept
my flat in seemingly good order.   I had heard a
great deal of the way proletarians used our homes :
the underwear hung up to dry on a string across the
drawing-room, the traces of dirty boots on the
Aubusson carpets, the silk hangings cut up to make a
skirt, books torn into cigarette paper. . . . I came
prepared for the worst, and was agreeably surprised
at the care the sailors had taken of my belongings.
The carpets had been cleaned, most things stood
in their old places ; big photographs of my daughter
adorned the tables.   The new owners, naturally,
ignorant of our true identities, were visibly dis-
pleased at our taking away the books, but the order
was official, the signature correct, our certificates
were regular.   So they had to comply.   I hoped I
would be able at the same time to gain access to my
writing-table and extract all letters, papers, and
souvenirs most dear to me.   But I failed.   The door
of my study was locked, the key, so they assured us,
had been taken away by one of their absent comrades ;
as to the papers, they had all been destroyed.   It
may have been true.   I dared not insist for fear of
arousing suspicion ; our situation, if discovered,

would have been disagreeable, to say the least of it.
The funny part of it was that the sailors imagined
themselves to be defending the interests of the absent
owner against us—the representatives of the Soviets !
. . . Life abounds in little jokes of the kind.   A pity
the public is for the most part utterly unappreciative.
It requires a greater detachment of mind than most
of us possess to enjoy the jokes life plays at our
expense.

I felt my throat contract and a mist float before
my eyes as the door of the flat closed behind us.
Shall I ever again see the English Quay, my rooms
looking out on to the Neva, the corner where we so
often sat in the gathering twilight, watching the
lights appear one by one on the other side, the
graceful outlines of the Imperial yachts standing
out clearly against the evening sky, and the black
shadows of the big, heavy barges gliding silently
down the river ?   Or will the years to come still find
me here, in this tiny house in a dirty little street
on the outskirts of Paris, with no other view but
the ever-drunken old coal-merchant opposite, and
workmen drinking their *apéritifs* in the pub at
the corner ? . . .

The books did not keep us going for long.   People
were too busy living to have time to read.   Books
fetch a low price on the revolutionary exchange.
All my beautiful library of medical works, collected
with so much care, went for practically nothing.

As to the kind gentleman from the Library Committee, all he took was *The Rape of the Lock*, illus-
trated by Beardsley, *Die Andere Seite*, by Kubin,
and Evreinoff's *History of Corporal Punishment*. He
could have taken all he liked. Let us hope his
modesty will be rewarded in Heaven, for he will
surely get nothing for it on earth.

And now our situation was getting desperate
again ; every single saleable object had been disposed of. Nothing remained but to take the course
I dreaded so much, and make use of my doctor's
diploma. I would naturally have done so long ago,
were it not for the Soviet decree obliging all doctors
under forty, women as well as men, to serve in the
Red Army. I was at that time still well under forty,
but having no desire to serve in the Army, I simply
did not register as doctor. This act of ' sabotage '
would, if discovered, bring down on me the dire
punishments threatened in the decree. All medical
activity seemed therefore to be ruled out. But I
had reckoned without my doctor friends. . . . One
of them put me in charge of a ward in a Red Army
Lazaret, another offered me a post as his personal
assistant in the surgical department of one of the
big hospitals. The Soviets had just before issued
an order compelling all doctors, in view of the
general shortage of medical aid in the city, to be on
the staff of three different Government institutions.
The absence of the usual method of transport, the

great distances, and the amount of work to be done, made this decree well-nigh impracticable. The authorities admitted, however, of no excuse. My third post was at the ' Petrocommune ', where it fell to me to supervise the prophylactic anti-cholera and typhus inoculation of all those employed in the bakeries of Petrograd.

In order to obtain meals we had to do as all the other inhabitants of the town, and join one of the communal refectories. Ours was fortunately in the house we occupied, which saved us the ordeal of having to stand for hours in a queue waiting for our rations. In a world full of misery, one annoyance the less was in itself a blessing. By relieving their misfortunes, however slightly, you can give people a temporary illusion of well-being. . . . But I am out to state plain facts and not to philosophize. Let the reader himself draw the necessary conclusions.

Those who came to dine at the ' Home of Arts ' mostly belonged to what used to be the brilliant Bohemian world of St. Petersburg. Nothing either brilliant or Bohemian remained, if by the latter epithet one understands the gay and care-free crowd as seen in the first act of Puccini's opera. Who would have recognized them now, the cream of the Russian intelligentsia, in that famished crowd, dirty and lice-ridden, silently devouring their miserable dinner ? The menu varied but little : a plate of thin soup with, swimming in it, a piece of vobla [1] head, and for the second course the perpetual dish of millet cooked in water. I had reached the stage when even the sight of millet sickened me ; I was simply unable to bear its sour, nauseating smell. . . . And the vobla was of course a hundred times worse.

How can I convey the real meaning of the word ' vobla ' to the mind of the European reader, for whom ' fish ' is naturally associated with the appetizing picture of *sole frite* or *turbot au vin blanc* ? What comparison shall I find to give with sufficient strength the repugnance of taste, smell, and even sight inspired by that meanest member of the whole ichthyological family ?   A mixture of bad egg with caster-oil, assafoetida with dog's bile. . . . No, my powers of description fail me ; they can only feebly portray the sickening horror with which my consciousness will for ever react to the word ' vobla '. Some readers will probably consider it ridiculous to speak of an insignificant detail like badly-tasting fish amidst the truly tragic events of those days. They will be right.   Only those who have been through it themselves know that the horror of rotten fish can in the long run overshadow even the horror of the guillotine.

The communal kitchens delivered no bread. Each district had its special centre for distributing bread to the holders of bread-cards. All the

[1] Vobla, a kind of fish.

bourgeois were classed under the third category and received one-eighth pound of black bread per day (and what poor bread at that !) As a doctor I was entitled to a pound a day, which is probably the only reason why I did not die of hunger.

My medical card had other privileges as well : once a month I was given a small piece of soap and a handful of sweets. Once or twice a year, a few yards of cloth, a bobbin of thread, maybe even a pair of boots. These little donations always came as a surprise ; one never knew beforehand what to expect. But this was only if one had the time and patience to visit many Soviet institutions, and could waste hours standing in various queues. Future text-books of history will probably single out this period as having witnessed the greatest absurdity into which the application of an abstract theory has ever led erring humanity.

In these circumstances numerous abuses were inevitable ; one was particularly amusing. The Soviets had decreed that the Government would present every bride with a few yards of dress-material ; those who made this law had doubtless forgotten the great ease with which marriages could be made and unmade in Soviet Russia. In a short time a whole class of women sprang up whose only occupation lay in extracting from the State as many yards of material as the number of their hastily-contracted and as quickly-dissolved marriages would allow. The decree had to be revoked : genuine

brides no longer received their new dress. Thus
are the innocent made to suffer for the sins of the
guilty.

The care of providing for our daily bread lay
entirely on my shoulders. Pierre was occupied by
another even more important matter—that of trying
to arrange for our departure. Otherwise we were
sure to perish—sooner or later.

The general social upheaval had, amongst other
things, played havoc with the well-regulated life of
the big town-hospitals. Having abolished all authority, the victorious proletariat saw no reason to make
an exception for the doctors. The nurses and
assistants, the maids and attendants had as much
common sense as the professors, and could surely
decide just as ably on the needs of the hospital.
Not content with intruding upon questions of
general management, they would often interfere
in purely medical matters ; the results were both
ludicrous and tragic. To take a case which occurred
to one of our doctors ; he told it me with tears in
his eyes. It had happened when he was getting
ready to perform an urgent operation on one of the
hospital attendants. The patient was on the table,
the assistant was just beginning the administration
of chloroform, when the door of the operating-room
flew open and several subordinate members of the
staff made their appearance. The delegation was
headed by the president of the local Soviet.

' We have decided that no operation is to take place.'

' But you are mad ! Don't you understand that it is a question of life or death for your comrade ? '

There was no way of reasoning with them.

' The committee has decided, and if you refuse to obey we will have to use force ! '

The voices became menacing ; a crowd of excited faces appeared in the doorway. . . . The doctor had to give in. By the time he had applied to the authorities, by the time the latter had investigated the case—the patient was dead.

Only people of great spiritual development were capable in such circumstances of continuing their work as before. There were a few such persons. We all know the name of the great scientist who through all those terrible years carried on undaunted his world-famous research-work. Such men deserve nothing but gratitude and admiration. I, alas, am not of the breed of heroes ! I took but a slight interest in my patients, did my work badly, and gave it as little of my leisure as was possible.

Some time during the revolution I had worked on the staff of one of the biggest hospitals for mental diseases in Petrograd. When shortage of food began to be felt in the city our patients were amongst the first to suffer. Wild cries filled the air of the whole building : the human animal was clamouring for food. Conditions grew from bad to

worse. The attendants, always brutal, seeing they
need no longer fear the doctors, turned into beasts.
If ever I entered a ward unexpectedly, I would find
several of the patients bound tightly to their beds,
their bodies covered with bruises, and marks of
blows on their faces. I was haunted for many days
by the mute pleading I had read in the eyes of one
young paranoiac ; on approaching him I discovered
that the ropes binding him had eaten so deeply into
his flesh that his whole arm was blue and swollen ;
he was in a state of such abject terror that he dared
not even complain, only his eyes spoke of the agony
he endured. . . . I shouted at the attendants, I
threatened, I pleaded. . . . I complained to the
head doctor. He shrugged his shoulders ; there
was nothing he could do. And the attendants only
laughed in my face, saying with studied insolence :
' It's not our fault, doctor ; the patients have been
fighting among themselves, so we had to interfere.'
They knew very well I did not believe a word of
it ; but they also knew that I was quite powerless
against them. A streak of sadism lies dormant in
nearly all of us ; given the circumstances, it will
raise its head, and the weaker the moral discipline
the easier will it conquer. No other period in
history (at least not in modern history) ever saw
such a triumph of all the lower instincts of man.
If once you adopt Lenin's slogan, ' Rob the robbers,'
there is no limit to where it may lead you. . . .

After a certain time I gave up psychiatry and

11

returned to my first passion—surgery. *On revient toujours à ses premiers amours.*

During that time Russian scientists wrote quite a number of learned articles concerning the influence of hunger on the human organism. They had at their disposal a vast field of observation. Every morning the dispensary was crowded with patients in all stages of starvation; some of them were bordering on collapse. Only these latter were admitted to the wards; it was impossible to have the whole population in hospital. As was inevitable in the circumstances, various epidemics soon developed; the number of those that succumbed daily to typhus, dysentery, etc., surpassed even the number of victims of motor accidents on festive days in New York. The chemists lacked even the simplest medicines; their supplies had been exhausted—new ones were unobtainable. It is, moreover, ridiculous to write out prescriptions when all that your patients require is food. Surgeons only consented to operate (unless the case was indeed an urgent one) after receiving definite assurance that during convalescence the patient would be supplied with food from home. It happened only too often that after a most successful operation the patient died on your hands from lack of nourishment; the wound refused to heal, the sutures went asunder. . . . We had quite a number of such cases.

At one moment the Government, to remedy a shortage of bread and other food, started the distribution of a considerable amount of raw oats. Those classes of the badly-famished population that possessed no means of cooking the oats began eating them as received—uncooked, uncleaned, and unground. The hospitals were soon full to overflowing. I myself observed several cases of complete obstruction of the whole intestinal tube, blocked with undigested grains of oats. The doctors were nonplussed ; our text-books mentioned no such cases. We tried everything : washings of the stomach, administration of purgatives, enemas. . . . Our patients kept on dying in the most horrible torment. Doctor Britske read us an interesting report at the surgeons' monthly meeting, ' On the Mechanical Ways of Cleaning the Rectum in Cases of Intestinal Obstruction Due to Raw Oats.' The death percentage was naturally very high. After a certain time the distribution of raw oats came to an end. The stock had probably been exhausted.

One of the effects of hunger consisted in a general cessation of the normal functions of the female organism ; women were no longer women. The birth-rate fell accordingly. Thus nature in her wisdom remedies the folly of man, and by keeping down propagation helps to save the race from destruction. The Government must have been satisfied ; a great deal of trouble and money were thus saved, which would otherwise have had to be spent in performing abortions on all those who lacked the vocation of motherhood.

One of the early measures of the Soviets had been to abolish all rights of succession. In the case of a patient dying in hospital all his belongings passed to the State. The wife demanding the money left in her dead husband's purse, the mother begging for the beloved one's watch or the ring he used to wear on his finger—all met with a refusal. They could cry their hearts out if they wanted. ' It is no use, madam. Such is the law.' All we could do was to adopt certain preventive measures. One hated having to explain to the old peasant woman, who had just brought in her son, all the gravity of his illness ; but we could at least insist on her leaving none of his things at the hospital.

' But why ? Why ? He'll need them when he gets better.'

' No doubt ; and you can bring them back when the time comes. For the present better do as you are told, and ask no questions.'

One night I was on duty in the Red Army Lazaret. About ten o'clock in the evening I was called to the telephone.

' Is that the doctor on duty ? Please come at once to the following address—my boy has been taken ill.'

' The doctor on duty is not allowed to leave the hospital.'

' But I insist on your coming immediately. The case is urgent.'

' Then bring the child here and I'll have a look at it.'

' I am the Commissar of the X district. If you refuse to come I will know what measures to take against you. What is your name ? '

That would not do at all. The last thing I wanted was to enter into conflict with some influential commissar.

' Wait a moment. I'll talk it over with the commandant of the Lazaret.'

The commandant, a quiet, uneducated man, was equally anxious to avoid alienating the mighty of this world.

' Better do as he wants, doctor. Let us hope nothing happens here in your absence.'

As was to be expected, the commissar's child had nothing but a slight cold ; or was it stomach-ache from overeating ? I really cannot remember.

I shall never forget one of my patients. He suffered from perforated appendicitis followed by diffuse peritonitis. He came too late to the operating table ; he was already past help. The man knew he was dying. But there was one thing he still desired, one last longing he wanted to satisfy before the end : once more to eat to his heart's content. It could have been no physical hunger ; his suffering body was in no state to require food. He would probably have been unable to eat the dinner had it been put at his bedside. The craving was purely psychological ; having gone hungry for so long, and knowing that food was at last within reach, he was determined not to let Death cheat him out of one last meal. ' Give me food ! Why don't you ? You know I am going to die. . . . A good plate full of kasha, with a big piece of butter and a cucumber. . . . Don't forget the cucumber. . . .' Probably no doctor on earth would permit such a meal to a patient with acute peritonitis. There are rules how men should live and rules how men should die. But we, in Soviet Russia, had so far lost all resemblance to human beings that even in the face of death we had no other wishes, no other thoughts but that of food.

A great many people took to drugs. Tchekists, sailors, and cinema actors were mostly addicted to cocaine. For some unknown reason the purveyors were generally barbers and hairdressers. Extraordinary as it may seem, they sold it comparatively pure, with hardly any admixture of sugar or soda. Young girls openly offered their friends a sniff. Quite shamelessly, in the street, they opened their hand-bags, took out their mirrors, as naturally as though to powder their noses. The medical class, as a whole, preferred morphia. As you left the hospital in the evening, after a hard day's work, the night nurse would laughingly offer you a box of ampoules : ' Take a sweet ? ' Even in this I had no luck : ' snow ' gives me palpitations of the heart, and morphine makes me sick, whilst the opium pipe, that gift of pagan gods to suffering humanity, was unknown in Russia. I had to look for consolation elsewhere. But where ?

Meanwhile, street urchins were selling ' typhuslice ' on the Nevsky, i.e. lice taken from the body of a typhus patient and liable to infect a healthy man.[1] For a few pennies you could buy a small matchbox with two or three parasites crawling on the bottom. The typhus epidemic was at its height ; the death rate about 50 per cent. No one thought it strange that there should be people desirous, of their own free will, of acquiring the terrible illness. One marvelled only at the great credulity of the purchaser ; how, indeed, could he distinguish the genuine ' typhus louse ' from the one the boy had only just caught on his own body ? As to the desire to fall ill—there was no mystery in that ; it was easy to imagine a situation which could only be avoided by a serious illness ; to escape being mobilized in the Red Army, to save oneself from imminent arrest, and so on. . . .

My way to the hospital led me nearly every day past the building of the Liteiny Commissariat, where eighteen months before Pierre and I had registered our marriage. It is a well-known fact that the Soviets have practically abolished all

---

[1] Typhus fever—*Typhus exanthematicus*—is transmitted through the bite of the louse.

formalities : a simple signature to declare one's willingness to contract the marriage, one's age, occupation, etc. Pierre described himself as ' philologist ', I called myself ' housewife '. One was also asked the family name one was going to adopt ; the husband could take the name of the wife, or the wife that of the husband, or each could retain his or her own name. Thus Pierre could have become Dolgorouky after my first husband, or Bobrinskoy after my father. It is hard to say why the thought should appear so utterly ridiculous. As we were leaving the Commissariat, Pierre's attention was attracted by an enormous red banner that hung across the room ; on it we read : ' She is awaiting him.' ' How sentimental,' exclaimed Pierre. ' It is probably the bride waiting for the bridegroom.' Then we came nearer and saw the full sentence : ' The *bourgeois* wants the guillotine. She is awaiting him.' [1] Under this emblem we laid the foundation of our new life.

Slowly, slowly, step by step, Pierre prepared the path that would lead us out of Russia. ' But, look here, everybody knows you are Russian and not Esthonian,' answered the Soviet officials to whom he applied for a passport. Day after day Pierre would return to the Commissariat for Foreign Affairs, situated in the building of the former

[1] In Russian ' she ' or ' he ' are often used in the place of the English ' it '.

Ministry where he had worked for so many years. He had left, together with the whole staff, in 1917, when the Bolsheviks came into power. Later, in the summer of 1918, a short time before our marriage, he had returned there in the hope of obtaining permission to go abroad ; we wanted to leave the country together and celebrate our marriage abroad. However, Fate had decreed otherwise. Pierre's application for a foreign passport resulted in his being put under arrest. The story of this first arrest is so extraordinary that I cannot resist the temptation of telling it, although it has no direct bearing on the events I am recording. I repeat it in Pierre's own words.

THE STORY OF PIERRE'S FIRST ARREST AS TOLD BY HIMSELF

Towards the end of July 1918 I applied to the Bolshevik authorities for a permit to go abroad, basing my request upon the necessity of safeguarding my belongings in Austria. In my capacity of First Secretary to the Russian Embassy, I had left Vienna (together with the other members of the Embassy staff) a few days after the declaration of war, leaving my flat with all the things it contained in the care of an Austrian lawyer. The day following my application the Tcheka paid me a visit. I was out when they came, so the search took place in my absence. On returning home I discovered that a great number of papers and letters had been taken. I at once telephoned to the Tcheka asking the reason of this search, and also for an answer to my request for a foreign passport. They told me to come to the Tcheka. I set out immediately. On arrival, I was received by one of the examining magistrates, who asked me a great many questions concerning my proposed trip abroad. After the interview he informed me that I was under arrest. I was then taken to a big room already crowded with prisoners. As the room contained no sleeping accommodation whatsoever, we had to pass the night as best we could. I slept on a table. Next day they took me to another smaller room, where I found several old friends. I remained here three days. New prisoners kept arriving, others were led away. On the last morning they brought in the Grand Duke Paul. I had not seen him for a long time and was very much struck by his worn-out appearance. He behaved with great calm and dignity, and one could see that even his jailers were impressed. He spoke to me with his usual amiability, recalling old times and our meetings abroad. That same evening I was transferred to the Shpalernaia Prison. A few days later the Grand Duke followed me. At the Shpalernaia Prison I also met the Grand Duke Nicholas Michailovitch. I am still in possession of a short note written by him telling me of some books in the prison library and signed ' Un des avant derniers Romanoffs '. I

passed ten days alone in my cell. Late in the
evening of the eleventh day I was conducted once
more to the Gorokhovaia. There I was kept
waiting for about an hour and a half. Towards mid-
night I was taken, together with ten other prisoners,
to be examined by Uritsky, the famous President
of the Petrograd Tcheka. My turn came last.

' You're a native of Esthonia ? ' was his first
question.

' As much as of Livonia, Kourland, Nijny-
Novgorod, Saratoff, Bessarabia. . . .' I answered,
naming all those Russian districts to whose nobility
our family belonged.

Uritsky then explained that the German Consulate
had interceded in my favour as an Esthonian. (This
unexpected intercession was due, as I learned later,
to the steps taken by Baron A. Meyendorff at the
Baltic Committee in Petrograd.)

' I know nothing about it,' I quite truthfully
answered him.

A short silence followed, then, looking me in the
eyes, he asked abruptly :

' You are naturally a Monarchist ? '

' I call myself an integral follower of the theocratic
principle,' was the answer I had carefully elaborated
during my ten days of solitary confinement.

' Explain your idea.'

' Well, the late Torquemada and the late Pobiedonostseff put the principle into practice, whereas
I am not active in doing so.'

' The principle that Pobiedonostseff applied was not theocracy but crude Russian autocracy. . . .'

I had not expected to find such an educated and clever adversary in the person of the all-powerful President of the Tcheka. Our conversation turned to the attitude adopted by the *bourgeois* classes towards the Soviet Government.

' You are yourself a member of the *bourgeoisie*,' said I, addressing Uritsky.

' Yes, I am probably more of a *bourgeois* than some of these officers here,' and he made a gesture towards the little group of prisoners that were seated at the farther end of the room patiently awaiting the end of my examination ; ' but we have joined forces with the proletariat.'

' You are a Don Quixote, but your political platform is not that of a Cervantes.'

' You are wrong. Don Quixote fought against windmills, whereas we are politicians in real life,' and Uritsky reminded me of the measures adopted by the Soviets to replace the old army officers by substituting men of a different standing in their place.

I answered him with the words I had once heard used by Richard Kühlmann, my former diplomatic colleague, and later head of the German Foreign Office :

' Glauben Sie mir, Fürst Wolkonsky, Kriege und Siege werden am grünen Tisch entschieden.'

' Nein, nein, nicht am grünen, am rothen Tisch,'

objected Uritsky, indicating the red cloth on the table before him. . . .

It was amusing to observe that Uritsky called me ' Prince ' several times in the course of this rather extraordinary conversation, the law by which the Soviets had proclaimed all titles non-existent having probably slipped his mind.

' Our conversation is very interesting, but the other prisoners are waiting,' said I, noticing the tired faces of my prison companions. It was past one a.m. The examination came to an end.

' And what about my passport ? '

' They will tell you upstairs.'

' Into whose hands, then, am I to commit myself ? '

' Go upstairs. You will be given all necessary instructions.'

An hour later I was free.

They had told me to return for my passport in a week's time. So precisely a week later I made my way to the Commissariat once more. I entered the building through the side door that faces on to the Moika, and following the long corridors I knew so well went along to the passport department on the second floor. On reaching my goal I discovered that the door of the room was closed. At the same moment I saw that the corridor contained quite a number of people standing about in small groups and talking excitedly. A few detached words reached me : ' He is dying . . . murdered . . .' I asked some one what had happened and learned that an attempt on Uritsky's life had just been made, at the main entrance. He was now lying downstairs at the point of death. Sentinels had been posted at all the doors, so that nobody could leave the building without a special permit. I was caught in a trap. Fully realizing the difficulties of my situation, I racked my brains for a means of escape, when by some lucky chance an old attendant, who had for years been attached to the Ministry, happened to pass along the corridor. I immediately led him aside.

' Can you tell me how I am to get out of here unobserved ? '

' The best way, your Highness, would be through the back stairs leading to the Moika. . . .'

The old man showed me the way, safely conducting me through a veritable maze of corridors and back stairs, the existence of which I had never even suspected.

The streets were already swarming with Tchekists on foot and on bicycles in hot pursuit of Kannegisser, the heroic executor of Uritsky. Those fearsome days of wholesale murder and mass executions, known as the days of the ' Red Terror ', were beginning.

CHAPTER V

I'm a creature that moves
In predestinate grooves,
I'm not even a bus, I'm a tram !

If a peer is sentenced to be hanged, he has the consolation of swinging by a silken cord.—WHITAKER'S PEERAGE.

RULERS who with one stroke of the pen abolish all old laws, old customs, old institutions, who with one sweep of the hand empty the whole past of a great country into the waste-paper basket of history, soon find themselves caught in their own snares. Every step they take presents the difficulty of a first step ; every act, however insignificant, is vested with the importance of creating a precedent.

It is quite impossible to relate all the trouble it cost Pierre to pave our way to freedom. Thanks to the help of his brother Grisha, and the kindness of the Esthonian Delegation, our certificates had at last reached us. Large sheets of paper, bearing the insignia of the Esthonian nobility, decorated with an imposing seal and signed by the President of the Council of Nobles, Von Lilienfeldt, stating that the bearer was a member of the princely family of Wolkonsky, with the title of Serene Highness, and belonging to the nobility of Esthonia.

175

Could one possibly present such a paper to the
Bolshevik authorities ? What would happen ? Would
not the whole building tremble with indignation,
would not the typists faint in dismay, Comrade
Zalkind ease his feelings by a string of choicest
oaths, and our frail hope of ever obtaining permits
to leave Russia be nipped in the very bud ?   In the
land of ' topsy-turvydom ' paradox is the rule,
whilst the most ordinary procedure is an object
of marvel.   The Government of ' Workers and
Peasants ', after having abolished alike titles, birth-
right, nobility, and even the name of Russia, now
bowed its head before the pompous paper of Herr
Von Lilienfeldt and included our names in the list
of Esthonians to be repatriated.   The first and most
difficult step had been achieved.   We had now to
wait for our turn to be given places in one of the
special trains that conducted across the frontier all
those who, like ourselves, were lucky enough to
belong to one of those Russian districts which the
revolutionary gale had for the moment detached
from the motherland.   In principle we were already
free.

From time to time the ' Home of Arts ' would
organize a reception.   Our rulers probably hoped
that the illusion of a ' feast ' would make us forget
the reality of the ' plague '.   When unable to feed
people, the best you can do is to try and keep them
amused : if not *panem* then *circenses*.   Quite a

number of visitors always attended these functions. It was here that I first met the well-known poet Gumileff, shot by the Bolsheviks about a year later. Here it was that we made friends with Prince Ouhtomsky, a charming, highly-cultured man, who likewise underwent the 'supreme penalty' for having communicated abroad some insignificant data concerning Russian museums. The English friends of the U.S.S.R. would here accuse me of exaggeration in vain : the sentence was officially published in the papers of the day, to the horror and dismay of those even who felt most leniently disposed towards the Soviets.

I wonder whether other people also experience that cold shudder down the spine every time they think of those friends and acquaintances who died a violent death ?   Not of those who fell gloriously on the field of honour with a bullet through the heart, but of those who perished at the hands of the executioner in some dark cellar of the Loubianka.[1] The black shadow of those last moments seems to be projected over their whole life on earth, as if the premonition of that coming horror must have tainted even the most happy and peaceful moments of their existence.   Why can I never think of our cousin Ivan Q., clever, amusing 'fat Ivan', without at once evoking the picture of those last hours when, after a whole night of torture at the

[1] The Loubianka, the head-quarters of the All-Russian Tcheka in Moscow.

12

hands of the unbridled soldiery, he stood facing the rifles of the firing-squad, the disdainful words on his lips : ' Brutes you have always been and brutes you have remained.' [1]   Why does the name of Princess Mary Stcherbatoff, whom I knew from childhood, make me think of nothing but that one moment when, stepping out of the door of her country-house, Bible in hand, to face the fierce crowd of peasants assembled for the purpose from all the neighbouring villages, she fell on the steps, her body riddled with bullets—killed by the hands of those same peasants whose well-being had been the chief care of her life.   Not content with murdering the mother they also killed her daughter, the beautiful, fair-haired Sandra, and would have done the same to her brother Dima had not he found a way to escape and to reach unobserved the cottage of his friend the forester—a false friend who, fearing the vengeance of the mob, seized a hatchet and smashed in the head of his young master.[2]

Is not their whole previous existence of greater importance and more value than these few short moments just before the end ?   Or, must we indeed

[1] I repeat the story the way I have heard it told.   I cannot, however, vouch for its accuracy.

[2] Those who directed the revolutionary movement from behind the scenes applied much fiercer measures against the good landlords than against the bad.   The latter could be of no danger to the new rulers, whereas there always existed a remote possibility of some peasants taking the side of those landlords they had loved and venerated for years.   The sooner they were put out of the way the safer the new-comers would feel on their usurped throne. . . . One more example of virtue bearing its own reward.

consider our whole life on earth as nothing but a
long preparation for the great mystery of Death,
and were the sages of antiquity right in advertising
their morbid saying, ' *memento mori* '—which, as
every one knows, means, ' Do not forget to die ' ?

People caught in an earthquake, as a rule, abandon
the occupation of the moment, and, obedient to the
law of self-preservation, flee from the scene of
danger.   If, however, the catastrophe, exceeding all
known limits of time, goes on for hours, days, and
even years, little by little people pick up the broken
threads of their existences, old habits reassert themselves, and a poor semblance of normal life is
re-established on the quivering soil. . . . Sometimes
we visited our friends, sometimes they would call
on us.   When I think of those days, a few faces
seem to stand out with exceptional clarity.   That
of Andrei Biely, mystical writer and dreamer, whose
association with the Bolsheviks seemed to our eyes
like one of those monstrous matings that so shock
the European mind when encountered elsewhere
than on the walls of an Eastern temple ;   that of
Piast, the eccentric poet, always hungry and dis-
hevelled, who used to come and share our miserable
supper, and read us the last chapters of his unpub-
lished novel. . . . Now and then we visited the old
Princess Soltykoff, who was quietly dying in the
two small rooms the Bolsheviks had left her at the
back of her house.   All Petrograd used to know the

pink-coloured house between the Champ de Mars and the Palace Quay—the pink house where we used to be taken as children to see the May Parade ; that in later years is associated in my mind with visits to the British Embassy and the clever, smiling eyes of O'Brien.[1] The pink house where. . . . But this is no place for sentimental reminiscences. And by now the pink house has probably long ago lost its original pink coating.

The same house also sheltered the aged Count Benckendorff and his wife. Brother of our Ambassador in London, *grand maréchal de la Cour*, he was one of the few who remained with the Tsar after his abdication. When the revolution broke out, only one out of all the personal adjutants of the Emperor, the Count Adam Zamoyski, came to offer the Empress his aid and sword. (True, most of them were then at the Front with their regiments.) Very few men in Russia thought the old cause worth fighting for. The reason for this must first and foremost be ascribed to ignorance ; had people known of the existence of a certain Vladimir Ilyitch Oulianoff (Lenin), they would have been ready to give up their lives not only for Nicholas II, but even for Ivan the Terrible. If only they had known !

Uncle Paul Benckendorff was a fine-looking old man, very tall, very lean, with old-fashioned manners

---

[1] Counsellor of the British Embassy ; he perished on the *Hampshire* with Lord Kitchener.

and a gentleman to his finger-tips. And she—but
what can one say of a mother who had just lost
both her sons in the most tragic manner? [1] The
younger one had been shot in Ekaterinbourg,
whither he had accompanied the Tsar ; the elder,
after many months of detention in various Soviet
prisons (for a time he had been together with Pierre),
had one day disappeared. ' He is here no longer,'
was the only answer the prison authorities deigned
to give his mother.   For over a year the old Countess
tried in vain to learn the truth.   ' Only let me know
whether he is alive or dead. All I beg of you is to
tell me whether you have shot him or not.' She
went to see Gorky, she wrote to Lenin. It was all
in vain. She kept on hoping for a whole year.
All through that nightmare year of 1920, with all
its hardships and physical privations, and the
repeated ' searches ' of their rooms by the Tcheka
which several times culminated in arrest and
imprisonment. When spring came their flat was
confiscated and they themselves turned out into
the street. The Countess had by now given up all
hope of ever seeing her son alive. The Bencken-
dorffs applied to the authorities for a permit to
leave Russia. Two old people—ruined, broken,
martyrized. You would expect even the Soviets
to let them go in peace. You think so ? You do
not know the Soviets. Day after day the old Count

---

[1] Princes Alexander and Vasily Dolgoroukoff, sons of Countess
Benckendorff by her first marriage.

toiled and worried, kept going from one Soviet institution to the other, from one official to the other. Always the same old story. Day after day . . . month after month. . . . In February 1921 they at last obtained their passports and left for Esthonia. No sooner had they crossed the frontier than the Count fell ill with pneumonia ; his exhausted body was unable to cope with the illness and he died a few days later in the quarantine hospital—at the very moment when he had at last reached the end of his trials, and the long-awaited freedom lay within reach. . . . He is buried at Fall in the family cemetery.

Those who are out to make a revolution can hardly afford the luxury of having human hearts.

' To-day I am celebrating my silver wedding with the Tcheka,' said Baroness Üxküll ; which meant that the Tchekists had that night searched her house for the twenty-fifth time.

The work I probably enjoyed most was vaccinating the staffs of all Petrograd bakeries against cholera and typhus. These vaccinations were compulsory, and were naturally considered by all those who had to submit to them as one more useless torment in their already miserable lives. In many cases the injection provoked a violent reaction, with fever, general sickness, and pronounced intestinal symptoms. Every individual had to be given two or

three injections at a week's interval. As a rule
no dispensation from work was granted. These
measures gave birth to a feeling of intense irritation
and bitter resentment towards their tormentors ;
all their long-accumulated hatred against the Communist Government was now directed against
myself, as representative of the Soviets. I never
imagined that being hated could give one so much
pleasure.

Besides, in every bakery I and the two nurses
under my orders were each given a freshly-baked
loaf of bread in compensation for our work : black
bread, Soviet bread—but still bread.

One of the privations that made me suffer most
was the impossibility of having a bath. Some (even
most) people seemed to regard it in the light of a
minor inconvenience. I did not know whether to
admire them for their indifference to physical discomfort or despise them for feeling no need for
bodily cleanliness : another example of the inconvenience of too careful an upbringing, which only
tends to develop an extra capacity for suffering and
renders one more vulnerable than the mass of
humanity to the blows of fate. After a month or
two of nothing but a small tub and cold water I
felt ready for even a communal bath. The usual
public baths had long since been abolished, but I
learnt somehow of the existence of a special *bania*
attached to the Alexander Theatre, where all artists

and theatre-workers could get a wash free. With
the help of some friends I obtained a ticket entitling
me to one wash in the *bania*.

It was my first visit to a communal bath, and I
sincerely hope it will be my last. How describe
it ? A medium-sized room, the air heavy with
steam and the exhalations of human bodies ; a
crowd of naked women standing in various postures
on the slimy, bespitten wooden floor ; some nonde-
script bloodstained rags and cast-off bandages lying
in an untidy heap in a corner. . . The room filled
with the noise of angry words and protests for a
place near the hot water tap or a vacant seat on one
of the benches. . . . . Hideousness and deformity in
every imaginable form and variety. . . . Underfed
bodies, meagre, pendant breasts, crooked legs, legs
swollen with oedema, legs with big knots of varicose
veins, like blue worms moving under the skin ; big
flat feet deformed by the ugly angles of inbent toes ;
backs covered with the bright dots of purulent boils,
marked by the red lines of itching scabies ; necks
and shoulders powdered with the pink patches of
syphilitic roseolas, innocently peeping out from
under the thick grey coat of dirt and lice of many
months' accumulation. . . . If hell exists, it surely
resembles that bathing-room of the Alexander
Theatre.

Pierre had been saved from a like ordeal by a
chance friend of his—a dancer in the former
Imperial Ballet. She asked him to her flat (artists

and ballet-dancers were privileged people in Soviet Russia) and let him have a few bucketfuls of hot water with which to wash in the kitchen.   In time of revolution a friend or two from the dancing world is a very necessary precaution.

The chief result of the absurd Communist experiment of which we were victims was to change ordinary everyday occurrences into difficult and often dangerous acts.   All the measures the Government had applied in its efforts to kill private trade had proved useless.   Not even the menace of death could change human beings into Communist robots, or stop the bartering and selling that was kept on round the old market-places.   The Russians had patiently allowed themselves to be despoiled of everything ; the only thing they would *not* give up was their right to buy and sell.   A strange people that values the freedom of commerce above the sanctity of the home, the integrity of their country above life itself.   A very strange people, indeed.

One day I nearly got caught.   As I was approaching the market of the Sennaia, the place was suddenly surrounded by soldiers, who without giving any warning began to shoot.   I cannot say whether they were aiming at the crowd or above the people's heads : I made my way home as fast as my legs would carry me.

The following small episode serves as an illustration of ' Our life in Russia in 1920 '.   We were

walking along the Kamennoostrovsky Street, Pierre
and I.   A little way ahead was a man with a big
sack of potatoes on his back.   Suddenly two big
potatoes slipped out of the sack and fell on to the
pavement, unnoticed by their owner, who calmly
continued on his way.   We reached the spot where
the potatoes lay in the mud.   The street was
deserted.   I looked at Pierre ; his face expressed
nothing.   I looked after the man with the sack and
had a glimpse of his back disappearing round a
corner.   The temptation was too great ; I bent
down, picked up the potatoes, deliberately wiped
off the mud with my handkerchief, and put them
into my pocket.

When in an irritated mood, Pierre sometimes
starts teasing me with ' People who pick their food
out of the gutter '. . . . Yes, I know he would
have sooner died than taken even a crumb that did
not legally belong to him, or stoop to gather anything
from the dirt in the street.   Therein lies his strength,
and my weakness.

My mother-in-law's health was visibly failing.
Her strength grew less every day and she spent
nearly all her time in bed.   Her once-clear brain
was unable to cope with the confusing events of
life.   On the day when Pierre had at last obtained
permits for us to leave Russia, he came happy and
proud to announce the good tidings to his mother.
Her first question was : ' Et Mathilde ? ' And when

Pierre patiently explained that Mathilde, being born in Finland, could not be included in the list of Esthonians awaiting repatriation, but would have to travel by way of Finland and would reach Fall nearly at the same time as ourselves, Mother-in-law's indignation knew no bounds : ' Comment !   Tu veux faire voyager ta vieille mère sans femme de chambre ?   Un bon fils n'aurait jamais fait cela. Penses-tu que Papa l'aurait jamais permis ? ' [1] (' Papa ' being her late husband, who had been dead for over twenty years.)   Pierre suffered deeply both from his mother's reproaches and from his own inability to comply with her wishes.

If only we had the means of procuring her enough food !   She once asked me to examine her legs. They were so much swollen with oedema she could hardly put on her stockings.   The sight of those pale, swollen legs, with deep depressions in the places where I applied my finger, haunted me for many weeks.   It was mainly a question of under-feeding.   We could do nothing.

When the weather allowed, the old butler and Mathilde seated her in a big arm-chair and took her out into the courtyard ; for an hour or two she would remain outside.   The whole house was, as I have said, occupied by the Bashkirs.   The soldiers, who kept moving about the yard, paid no attention

---

[1] ' What !   You want to force your old mother to travel without her maid ?   A dutiful son would never do such a thing.   Do you imagine Papa would have allowed it ? '

to the lonely old woman quietly sitting there in her big, old-fashioned hat and black silk mantilla.

It happened on a fine afternoon, a short time before the day fixed for our departure. Mother-in-law was sitting as usual in the courtyard, enjoying her hour out of doors. The yard was suddenly filled with commotion : strangers had appeared and were opening the shed where Mother-in-law kept her carriages. One by one the huge old monsters were pulled out into the open.

'What is the matter ? Why have they opened the shed ? '

'Do not be anxious, your Highness,' shouted the old butler into her ear ; ' they've come to requisition the carriages.'

It seemed difficult to understand that any one should need those big, heavy vehicles, relics of past days ; they were so utterly unadapted to the needs of the revolutionary proletariat, these carriages in which ten years ago an aged princess made the round of her friends, accompanied by a footman in livery seated on the box next to the coachman. The only place for them would be in some historical museum.

The old warlike spirit had awakened in Mother-in-law's breast.

'They have no right to my carriages. I am a native of Esthonia. Mathilde, go upstairs and bring me my Esthonian papers ! '

She knew of course that she would never have

the smallest use for those carriages ; there could
be no question either of selling them or of taking
them to Esthonia ; in a few days they would be
abandoned to whatever fate awaited them.

'Your Highness, it is safer not to start any
discussion. . . . There may be complications. . . .'

Nothing could stop her.

'Mathilde, do as I tell you.'

The men who had come for the carriages were
very much astonished at encountering such unexpected resistance. True, Esthonians had the right
to take their belongings with them. But did she
really imagine she'd be allowed to take these big,
heavy carriages into the train as her personal
luggage ? She would listen to none of their arguments. Because of her deafness she probably
missed the greater part of what they said.

'These are *my* carriages, and you dare not touch
them ! '

First they argued, then they cursed. . . . Then
they gave it up and took themselves off. The
carriages remained in the shed.

Il n'y a qu'un pas du ridicule au sublime.

The day fixed for our departure was drawing
near. It seemed too good to be true. We lived
in fear of some untoward event, some unforeseen
circumstance coming to change the minds of our
rulers and shatter our hopes. Would they really
let us go ? Twice we were on the brink of disaster

The first time was when I fell ill with dysentery. As I now write it, the word does not look at all terrible. At that time it was different; every day several cases of death from dysentery were registered. Doctor Silberthal did not mince matters and told Pierre straight out that he must not count on my recovery; only the day before he had been to the funeral of a lady colleague who had died from dysentery; she was of my age. Useless to cherish illusions. The first thing to do was to take a good dose of castor oil.

Soulless things are as merciless in their revenge as human beings. Castor oil—the greatest enemy of my childhood! How I would have laughed at the thought that one day I would be vainly praying for a drop of the precious liquid!

Pierre made the round of all the chemists in Petrograd; castor oil was not to be had for any money. (It was not that the whole town suffered from indigestion; but being short of butter, the population had little by little eaten up all the castor oil obtainable. To think of a dinner prepared on castor oil! Is there anything more degrading than a revolution?)

Dear Doctor Nopolshina! If ever you come across these lines, know that I have not forgotten the small bottleful of the priceless oil you brought me that day. It is a debt I shall never be able to repay.

Was my quick recovery due to the castor oil or

to the fact that I had still to expiate on earth the
sins of some previous incarnation ? Whatever the
reason, a few days later I was once again on my feet.

The mental strain of those last few days was
unimaginable. We breathed an atmosphere of
tension like that of the sick-room ; we lived so to
speak on tiptoe, fearful lest some loud word or
careless movement should provoke a catastrophe.
The nearer we drew to the day of departure the
greater grew the tension. The acrobat crossing
Niagara on a tight rope must experience the same
feeling when only a few steps remain between him
and firm land. Just before the end an incident took
place that very nearly sent us all whirling into the
abyss.

I have already mentioned my work in one of the
Red Army Lazarets. The two wards in my care
held about twenty patients, mostly light cases. I
usually left my work at the Lazaret to the last,
arriving there towards the end of the day ; my work
finished I would hurry home. The routine work
consisted of an inspection of all patients, the writing
of necessary prescriptions, and dressing of wounds.
Once a week I accompanied the head doctor in his
visit, receiving from him general directions concerning the more serious cases. Of course I could
always ask his advice in case of difficulty. Thus it
came about that I hardly ever met the other doctors
who worked in the same establishment ; several of
my colleagues I had never even seen.

That day I had worked in the Lazaret longer than usual, and, being in a hurry to get home, felt quite annoyed on discovering that some one had locked the cupboard in the doctors' room where we were in the habit of leaving our things. I had no wish to go without my hat, so in an irritated voice I called the maid :

'Masha, come here at once. Why have you locked the cupboard ? '

' It's not my fault, doctor. It's Doctor Sobso-vitch who locked the cupboard and took the key with her to the operating-room.'

' Then please go and get me the key. Tell Sobsovitch my things are inside, and that I have no time to lose.'

Under my breath I added a few disparaging remarks concerning people who know no better than to treat the communal cupboard as it if were their own.

In a few minutes Masha reappeared with the key and I hastily unlocked the cupboard and took out my things. Then, having locked the cupboard once more, I gave the key to Masha to be returned to Doctor Sobsovitch, and decided to lodge a complaint against her the next time I saw the head doctor. Personally, I had never in my life met Doctor Sobsovitch, had never before so much as heard her name.[1]

[1] Sobsovitch is her real name—at least the name by which she was then known. You can never be sure with a Bolshevik what name he

From the Lazaret I went straight home—meaning by ' home ' the former study of M. Elisseeff.   The day had been a strenuous one and I felt exceedingly tired ;   throwing off my shoes I lay down on my bed to enjoy *Le parfum de la dame en noir* which some kind soul had just lent me.   Strange how a good story is often so much more absorbing than real life (love stories excluded, of course).   Here was I, in the midst of happenings so fantastic that no author would have ever dared imagine them, here was I looking for a thrill in the pages of one of the minor French novelists.

I had just become thoroughly engrossed in the extraordinary adventure of Rouletabille when a knock came at the door of the dressing-room.   Pierre opened and saw before him an unknown lady and a Red Army soldier ;   he, pale, confused, and obviously sheltering behind his companion, a good-looking, dark-haired woman of a flashy Jewish type, loud-voiced and with bold, even aggressive, manners.

' I am Doctor Sobsovitch,' said she, ' and this is Comrade Fedoroff, Commandant of the Lazaret. I want a few words with Doctor Wolkonsky.'

Without waiting for an invitation, she pushed herself past Pierre into the room.   I showed her into the study, while Pierre remained with the commandant in the dressing-room.

' A most disagreeable thing has happened,' began

will be going by next time you meet him.   As the reader will see, the woman had reason enough to wish for a new name.

13

Sobsovitch as soon as she had taken a seat. ' I have lost my diamonds.'

' What a terrible misfortune ! How did it happen ? '

' It happened to-day in the Red Army Lazaret. I had the stones in my portfolio, and whilst I was at my work they disappeared.'

I was still far from guessing the real meaning of her words, and was profuse in the expressions of my sympathy. I did not quite grasp why she had come for comfort to me, a complete stranger, but attributed it to the distraction into which her loss had thrown her.

With a few concise words she disillusioned me.

' Yes, Colleague Wolkonsky, and I suspect you of having taken them.'

' What ! '

The first reaction was one of surprise. I felt neither anger nor indignation—only astonishment. A bomb bursting at my feet, the Mikado entering my rooms in full glory, could not have surprised me more. . . .

' What ! What did you say ? '

She calmly repeated her accusation. Was the woman mad ?

I called Pierre out of the next room. Once more, in his presence, she accused me of having stolen her diamonds. Pierre went pale.

' Your being a lady obliges me to control myself.'

Sobsovitch remained quite unconscious of his

thrust. She told us that she had already rung up the Criminal Department of the Tcheka—the so-called Ugrosysk—and demanded that Pierre and I should return with her to the Lazaret. We had no choice but to comply; refusal would have been worse than useless and would only have strengthened whatever case there might be against us. Moreover, we were naturally anxious that the mystery should be cleared up without any delay.

On our way to the Lazaret I tried to put my thoughts in order. To begin with, diamonds were a curious object for a lady doctor to keep in her portfolio. What struck me as even more important was the fact that time and again the Soviets had issued decrees proclaiming the confiscation of all precious stones, gold, and silver in possession of private individuals. Those who did not deliver them at once to the authorities were threatened with severe punishment. How was it, then, that Sobso-vitch not only openly proclaimed her ownership of these forbidden articles, but even applied for help to the Tcheka ? Why did she not fear punishment for having kept them contrary to the law ? She accused me of having stolen her diamonds. Now that I thought it over, the whole absurdity of the accusation became clear. How could I, who had never in my life seen either Sobosvitch or her port-folio, have guessed the importance of its contents, picked it out from amongst the belongings of all the other doctors, and removed the valuables in

14

those few short moments while the key was in my possession, and under the very eyes of the maid (who stood waiting to return it to Sobsovitch). Any unprejudiced person would be bound to see the impossibility of the situation. But would my judges be unprejudiced ? The fact that Sobsovitch had at once telephoned to the Tcheka, without even informing the head doctor and director of the Lazaret, was in itself suspicious. Extremely suspicious. The vast majority of Russian citizens feared nothing so much as the Tcheka, and would, on no pretext whatever, willingly apply to it. The haste with which Sobsovitch sought help from that universally abhorred institution showed her to be in some special way connected with it. There seemed to be a sinister meaning behind the whole incident. The inevitable conclusion to be drawn was that Sobsovitch was an agent of the Tcheka, and that this was some deep-laid plot—a device to search our rooms and confiscate whatever riches they hoped to find, without in any way offending the susceptibilities of the Esthonian Government that had taken us under its protection.

By this time we had reached the Lazaret. The Tchekists were there waiting for us. I was separated from Pierre, conducted by two Tchekist women to a room and stripped of my clothing. Every single garment was carefully examined for the ' missing diamonds '. Pierre was subjected to the same ordeal in a neighbouring room. You can of course try and persuade yourself that the wild bull which throws you into the mud, the mad dog that chases you into the mire, the Tchekist who forces you to undress cannot humiliate your self-respect. You can tell yourself all that and much more ; but I am sure that Coué himself would have required a course of special training in the art of auto-suggestion to make this belief take firm root in his mind under such circumstances as these. Even now, after more than ten years, something of that impotent rage and that sense of humiliation awake again in me as I picture myself standing half-naked under the prying eyes of those women. And when I think of Pierre, my hand gropes for a revolver.

Convinced that no diamonds were hidden in our clothing, the Tchekists next repaired to our room in the Home of Arts. The search took four hours —from nine in the evening to one in the morning. They explored everything, investigated every corner, even to the smallest chink where a few small stones could possibly be concealed. Doctor Sobsovitch took an active part in the performance. I knew, of course, that they would find nothing ; we had neither money nor precious stones left, either hidden or unhidden. But when you have to do with the Tcheka, you never know what surprise may be in store. I tried not to miss a single one of their movements. At one o'clock in the morning the search ended. Their hopes of laying hands on the riches we had put aside in view of our imminent departure had been frustrated. They were forced to admit we had nothing.

'And now, Citizeness Wolkonsky,' said the very young man who seemed to be head of the party, 'I am obliged to arrest you.'

'But you have not discovered anything in our rooms! You have no reason for arresting me.'

'Citizeness Sobsovitch would not accuse you without reason.'

No more doubts could remain concerning the role of Sobsovitch in the affair. However, I was prepared to fight for my liberty.

'Look here. You cannot put a person in prison on such a slight suspicion. Your accusation is in itself absurd; in the circumstances, it would have been simply impossible to steal any diamonds out of that portfolio under the very eyes of the maid. . . .' ('Admitting that they ever existed, which I very much doubt,' I added under my breath.)

'Given a certain dexterity of the fingers, the feat is possible,' was the insolent reply.

The Commandant of the Lazaret, until then a silent witness of the proceedings, now took my part; even his slow brain must have grasped that there was something wrong about the whole affair. He evidently belonged to that rare species, an honest Communist. The Tchekist gave in and contented himself with my written promise not to leave Petrograd without authorization.

Our situation was still highly precarious. We

were probábly saved by the unanimous protests
that reached the Tcheka from all sides. Hardly
was the door shut behind the intruders than the
inhabitants of the Home of Arts assembled in our
rooms.   (The Tchekists were supposed to have gone
to search Sobsovitch's room and to look among her
own things for the missing stones. As we learned
later, they never reached their destination but
turned back half-way ; there was no need for them
to search one of their own agents for a treasure that
never existed outside of their imagination.) Notwithstanding the lateness of the hour, nearly all the
inhabitants of the Home of Arts had crowded into
our room to express their sympathy. Some one
suggested writing a protest to the head of the
Ugrosysk. They at once proceeded to compose a
letter to be signed by names well known in the
world of Russian literature and arts. It was a long
letter, elaborately styled, expressing the profound
indignation they all felt, and stating that ' Doctor
Wolkonsky is a highly respected comrade of ours,
and to suspect her of having taken any one's diamonds is as ridiculous as it would be to accuse the
celebrated author Korolenko of stealing a pair of
silver spoons. . . .' I was deeply touched.

The next day a like protest, only shorter and in
a simpler style, was addressed to the Tcheka by my
hospital colleagues. It was signed by the whole
staff, including the nurses, assistants, and attendants
—whose support was of course of much greater

weight than that of the doctors and the scientists.
Greatest of all was the indignation aroused in the
Lazaret itself ; here also the whole staff took my
side.

The Tcheka had not expected such a unanimous
outcry in my favour. I was only once called up
before the examining magistrate. The first person
I met on entering the building was—Sobsovitch.
On catching sight of me she hastily disappeared.
And that was the end of the whole story so far as
I was concerned. Sobsovitch, however, got pun-
ished for her misdeed : the doctors of the Lazaret
refused to have any further dealings with an un-
masked Tcheka agent and demanded that she should
leave. They all feared the same thing would next
happen to them. Doctor Arenstein put down in
big letters on the first page of his note-book ' Cave
Sobsovitch '. That was the general attitude. Both
Sobsovitch and I were present at the general doctors'·
meeting at the Lazaret that took place a few days
later. We passed each other with no sign of
recognition. I do not know what her feelings were,
but I would rather have shaken hands with a
crocodile ; possibly she felt the same. My satis-
faction was complete when I heard some of the
things the head doctor told Sobsovitch to her face.
I nearly felt sorry for her ; nearly—not quite. I
am no sweet forgiving nature.

After it had all blown over and no danger threatened us any more, Pierre could not resist the

temptation of teasing me : ' Now, won't you confess where you have hidden the diamonds ? '

The day came. The day of our departure. Some friends had kindly unearthed a motor-car to convey Mother-in-law and her luggage to the station. The old butler, also a native of Esthonia, was going by the same train with his wife and daughter. Pierre and I had also been given a car—a big car belonging to the Commissariat of the Navy and obtained through some friends of Larissa Reisner, the mistress of the famous sailor Raskolnikoff, who was commander of the Soviet fleet. The two sailors on the front seat gave the car a distinctly military appearance ; those who saw us probably pitied us for being under arrest. In Soviet Russia appearances are more deceptive than anywhere else.

We arrived at the station many hours before the train was due to leave : necessity, not *Eisenbahnfieber*. On one of the side platforms stood a long train made up of trucks : that was our train. The platform was swarming with people, all heavily loaded, shouting, pushing, dragging their various belongings. There is no sight so desolate and so ugly as that of a train of repatriates—repatriates from Soviet Russia. All the accumulated rubbish of years, the useless things that had been lying unheeded in some dark corner of the house, some dusty attic, or mouldy cellar were now pulled into the open, shamelessly displayed to the light of the sun.

Objects strange and unexpected met the eye : a
broken parrot-cage next to a bicycle without wheels ;
an armless pierrot seated on what was left of a rich
fur coat ; basins that had lost their enamel coatings ;
a chair without back ; an umbrella without a
handle. . . . As to the persons to whom these
things belonged, the less said about them the better.
Three years of Bolshevism had been enough to
turn these once normal people into the caricatures
of human beings, terrorized, degraded, and warped
both physically and mentally, that are called ' Soviet
citizens '. Foreigners who witnessed the arrival of
such a train at Narva no longer asked how it was
possible for a country of a hundred and forty million
people to bear the yoke of a handful of Communists.
They had understood. And that, notwithstanding
the fact that the repatriates were the happiest, not
to say the only happy, people in Russia ; they had
won a bigger prize than the Calcutta Sweep—
permission to leave the country. Never in all my
life have I seen such fierce envy as that which
burned in the eyes of the friends to whom I said
good-bye before going abroad. Had it been possible
to escape from the Soviets with the help of a self-
inflicted wound in the hand, the way a few cowardly
soldiers eluded the trenches during the war, all
Russia would be to-day without fingers. Alas !
freedom could be bought only by the sacrifice of
one's head.

We were now faced with the problem of getting

Mother-in-law into the train. No stretchers were
to be had, so we helped her into an arm-chair,
carried her to the train, and then with the help of
a dozen strong men succeeded in lifting the heavy
chair into the cattle-truck in which we had been
given places. On the floor at one end of the truck
we placed an air mattress, covered it with blankets,
surrounded it with cushions, and laid down our
invalid. After a great deal of rearranging of the
cushions we succeeded in making her fairly comfortable. It was, in any case, the best we could do.
The removal had badly taxed her strength. Her
emaciated face, with its yellow-tinted skin and great
pouches beneath the eyes looking out from under a
heavy black hat, her thin body wrapped in a dark
fur coat, the trembling hands and vague questioning
glances, were terrible to behold. In those days
people were used to many a sad and gruesome
sight, but on seeing her the passers-by shuddered
and hastily averted their eyes. . . .

We were not the only passengers in the truck.
Besides the butler and his family there were also
three or four strangers. Our luggage occupied but
little space : a small box, two or three suit-cases
with some worn-out linen and a few old dresses—
that was all.

Hour after hour of waiting. No one knew at
what time the train would start. Pierre kept pacing
nervously up and down the platform. Nerves are
catching ; stories of people detained at the very

last minute kept running through my mind. In which column of the great book of statistics would we be inscribed ? Of those that had succeeded or of those that had failed ? Only on the other side of the frontier would we be in safety.

Evening came and still nothing happened. It grew dark, a fine drizzling rain began to fall. We sat silently, in a state of dull somnolence, with neither thought nor feeling, only waiting, waiting. . . . Would the end never come ?

Some one ran down the platform, a command rang out, then a shrill whistle and the train started : first slowly, then quicker and quicker. We were moving. Could it really be true ?

There is many a slip between the city and the frontier. Were our sufferings still too light to balance the scales of Justice ? Hadn't we yet earned our freedom ? Or had the devil been granted permission to take us through one last ordeal ?

About four or five miles from the town the train slowed down and then stopped altogether. What was the matter ? Complete darkness reigned outside ; it was pouring with rain. We could see nothing—nothing but a deep ditch at our feet and the vague outlines of untilled fields beyond.

The figure of a man with a lantern in his hand came running along the train ; he was shouting something. As he came nearer we could distinguish the words : ' The last ten trucks are not going any farther. All passengers are requested to take their places higher up.' At first we did not understand. It took us some time to grasp the terrible fact that our truck was the last but one.

It was more than a calamity—it was a disaster. The other trucks were all full, and it would have been no easy task to find places for us and for our luggage. Still, it could have been done, had it not been for the one insurmountable obstacle—my Mother-in-law. To transport her from one truck to another without a stretcher, or even an arm-chair, was simply impossible. To jump from the high truck down into the darkness, the rain, the deep ditch below us, to pass the whole length of the train and to climb high up into another truck, was no easy task even for a young and healthy being. As for Mother-in-law, who could hardly move without help, the whole thing was absolutely out of the question. What then? If we remained in the car, we would be taken back to Petrograd—a Petrograd with nowhere to go to, with our rooms already occupied by new-comers, with nothing to eat, no money to live on, with Mother-in-law on our hands and the prospects of a new departure uncertain. It was too awful even to contemplate. It was the end of everything.

In all our life together I have never seen Pierre so upset as at that moment. He forgot the rain, forgot his hat, jumped off the car and ran in search of the train commandant. The latter proved to be an amiable Esthonian gentleman who would have been glad to help us but was quite powerless to do so. The engine, it appeared, was not sufficiently powerful; the train would either remain stuck where it was or else some of the trucks would have to be left behind. . . . Pierre was frantic. He argued, prayed, begged the Esthonian in the name of his own mother. . . . Despair rendered him eloquent. The man could not resist him. He ran off, consulted some one, got the necessary permission and came back to tell Pierre that our car would be attached to the train. Pierre returned to us drenched to the skin, the water running down his face, his whole body trembling with excitement. But the battle had been won.

The manœuvring began. Our car was moved up and down, first one way, then the other. We strained our eyes, peering into the darkness, trying to guess the meaning of each separate jolt; our brains were paralysed with the sickening fear of being left behind. Mother-in-law had caught the general excitement : ' Petia, Petia, que se passe-t-il ? Qu'est ce que vous regardez tous les deux ? ' Vainly we tried to soothe her.

One last movement of the truck : backwards . . . forwards . . . the clash of iron as we joined another car. . . . Now we were being attached to it, now the train was moving once more . . . moving in the right direction. Was it only another manœuvre ?

For some time now the train had been travelling

steadily in the direction of Yambourg. But our
nerves were still quivering ; every lessening of speed
seemed to announce a stop, to be followed by the
dreaded journey backwards ; every whistle seemed
to portend disaster. . . .

On the second day we reached the frontier. With
every hour the tension grew more strained. Nerves
were stretched to breaking point. Mother-in-law
was restless. Every few minutes she would call :

' Petia ! Petia ! '

' Que veux-tu, Maman ? '

' Combien de degrès y-a-t-il dehors ? '

' Je ne sais pas, il fait assez frais.'

' Il n'y a pas de thermomètre à la fenêtre ? '

' Mais non, voyons, Maman, tu sais bien que
nous sommes dans un wagon de marchandises.'

The words were drowned in the noise of the
wheels, and had to be shouted at the top of the
voice. For a few minutes she would be quiet, then
it would begin all over again :

' Petia, Petia, viens ici.' . . .

His patience was boundless ; whatever his occupation, whether he was lying down or had just
taken up a book, in a moment he was at her side.

' Tu m'as appelé, Maman ? '

She was very old, very ill and feeble, and, as
often happens in such cases, very exacting.

We had still the frontier before us—the last and
probably the most terrible obstacle of all ; customs
examination of luggage and of people, inspection of

papers and documents. We had all heard of people turned back from the frontier because of some trifling irregularity, a small infraction of the rules. Some of them, as we knew, had been led straight to prison.

The personal examination included cutting open of coat linings, searching in the hair and beneath the dress. I was asked to take off my boots. A woman next to me was sobbing wildly ; the precious stone she had hidden in the heel of her shoe had been discovered and taken from her ; her own fate was still uncertain.

Mother-in-law had been allowed to remain in the truck : even the Tchekists were impressed at sight of her. The woman they sent in to search her did her work in a most perfunctory way ; even she lacked courage to lay hands on such an invalid. Later we learnt that all the while Mother-in-law had kept three gold coins secreted on her person. All her life she had been in the habit of giving a certain sum of money to the priest on the celebration day of the chapel at Fall. Nothing, not even a revolution, would keep her from performing the traditional gesture. She probably never realized, never even stopped to think of the terrible danger that would have threatened all of us, and herself above all, had her ruse been discovered.

The search was ended, our papers examined. Everything went off smoothly. We had been allowed to pass. There followed a long period of waiting. Never, never in all my life had the minutes passed so slowly. It was many times worse than waiting for the results of a school examination, worse than waiting for a late sweetheart, or for the pangs of child-birth to come to an end. Every second was an eternity. Would the train never start ? . . . Should we be allowed to cross over to the other side ?

We could neither read, nor talk, nor even think. The man in the dock, on trial for his life, waiting for the verdict, will be unable to tell you what are his thoughts while the jury consider their decision. There are probably no coherent thoughts in his head; all ideas are drowned in the one tense expectation, the one terrible question : yes or no ? Yes or no—will they let us go ?

Every torture comes to an end. A whistle, a small jolt. The train starts—slowly, slowly, nearer and nearer to the frontier. . . .

A small muddy river. A few armed soldiers. A bridge. . . . I look at Pierre ; but he is not looking at me. His glance is directed back, from where we had come, back—into Russia. . . . Now he makes the sign of the cross. We are in Esthonia.

I fall on my knees, my face in my hands. Sobs are stifling me. . . . From the corner come the trembling sounds of an old voice :

'Petia ! Petia ! Sommes-nous arrivés ? '

AFTERWORD

'WELL, and what next?' some one may inquire. Next? Next came our life in Europe, great expectations and even greater disappointments. . . . My own carelessness, other people's meanness. . . . Money, ruin, poverty. . . . Giving gymnastic lessons, acting in a cinema studio, reading aloud to an old banker, nursing in a clinic in Nice, driving a taxi in the streets of Paris. . . .

The bitter fruits of defeat.

INDEX

Abo, 29
Afonassieff, Mrs. Elena Niko-
laievna, 90, 105, 114–115,
146
Aguerra, 7, 17
Arenstein, Dr., 200

Bath, 8
Behr, Nicholas, 17, 18
Benckendorff, Count Constan-
tine, 110, 113, 114, 132
Benckendorff, Count and Coun-
tess Paul, 180–182
Biely, Andrei, writer, 149, 179
Bobrinskoy, Count, house of, 81,
148
Britske, lady doctor, 163

Crimea, 2, 3, 8, 9

Demidoff, Elisabeth, 19
Dolgoroukoff, Prince Alexander,
111, 181
Dolgoroukoff, Prince Vasily, 181
Dolgorouky, Princess Olga, 2, 8,
9, 10, 11
Dolgorouky, Princess Sophy, 2,
8, 9, 11
Dzerjinsky, head of the All-
Russian Tcheka, 89, 136,
142, 143

Elena Nikolaievna. *See* Afonas-
sieff, Mrs.
Enoukidze, secretary of the
V.C.I.K., 130, 132
Ermoloff, Mr. and Mrs., 144
Essenin, poet, 112

Fall, the Wolkonsky family place
in Esthonia, 36, 134, 135,
182, 208
Fehleisen, Baron and Baroness,
144

Golitsin, Princess Paul and
family, 144

Gorky, Maxim (Alexei Maksi-
movitch Peshkoff), 77, 78,
86, 97, 98, 101, 116, 131
Goudovitch, Count Alexander,
111
Gumileff, poet, 177

Home of Arts in Petrograd, 148,
176, 197

Ignatieff, Count Alexei Nicolae-
vitch, 44, 46, 49, 50, 53
Ilyin, Professor, 117
Ivan Adamovitch. *See* Sepper

Kalinin, President of the
U.S.S.R., 130
Kamenev, Bolshevik Commissar,
119, 130
Kannegisser, 174
King, Miss, 9, 12
Kotzebue, Alexander, 140, 141
Krassikoff, Bolshevik Commis-
sar, 114, 115, 118, 128, 129
Krassin, Bolshevik Commissar,
13, 14, 25, 98–101, 114, 129
Kronstadt, 3, 6, 98

Mannerheim, General Baron, 5,
19, 20
Marie Feodorovna, Dowager
Empress, 8
Marsh, General, 31
Mathilda, 74, 187
Meyendorff, Baron Alexander,
171
Meyendorff, Baron Lulik, 44
Mouravieff, Valerian, 117

Nadejda Amandovna, 105
Narva, 44
Natasha, 82, 83
Newcastle, 15
Nicholas Mihailovitch, Grand
Duke, 170

211

Printed by Jarrold & Sons Ltd. Norwich

For Product Safety Concerns and Information please contact our EU
representative GPSR@taylorandfrancis.com
Taylor & Francis Verlag GmbH, Kaufingerstraße 24, 80331 München, Germany